Iky's Bipolar World

by
Randy Cassatt

Order this book online at www.trafford.com
or email orders@trafford.com

Most Trafford titles are also available at major online book retailers.

Printed in Victoria, BC, Canada.

ISBN: 978-1-4269-2039-4

*Our mission is to efficiently provide the world's finest, most comprehensive book publishing
service, enabling every author to experience success. To find out how to publish your book, your
way, and have it available worldwide, visit us online at www.trafford.com*

Trafford rev. 12/03/09

www.trafford.com

North America & international
toll-free: 1 888 232 4444 (USA & Canada)
phone: 250 383 6864 ♦ fax: 812 355 4082

Introduction

When I began writing this book, it started out as a form of therapy. I found out I had Manic-Depressive Disorder when I was forty years old. I became disabled because of it when I was forty-three years old. When I was born, I also had nerve deafness, so I couldn't hear very well. This book is full of my own personal experiences through the years, some fiction, and the combination of both. Many of these jokes I wrote while I was having manic episodes. I have always believed that laughter is the best medicine, and as my good friend A.J. said, "Misery loves company."

This book is dedicated to everyone who suffers from some form of mental illness or disability because of it. I have never tried to benefit from or use my disabilities to gain things. They are my assets, not liabilities, to carry on and prove that I am just as good a person as anyone else is. We have to face the facts that we live in a very cruel world today where lies, manipulation, cheating, stealing, harassment, and hostile environments are very commonplace.

As you read this book, some of these jokes may offend you. Just think of the saying that we have in Arkansas, "If you don't like the weather, just wait a couple of days and it will change." The same goes with these jokes. If you read a joke that you don't like, just read on and they will change. You can't please everybody so all you can do is try to please yourself!

When I was a little boy, my Dad looked at me and said, "You look like a Jew and your nickname is Iky the Jew." Looking back now, I think that my Dad somehow knew that I was going to have a rough life, and he knew that a Jew could take it. I remember one time when Dad was scolding me about something I had done, and I told him, "I wasn't asked to be brought into this world." Dad looked at me and he said, "Neither was I."

My whole purpose of this book is to make the reader laugh. Maybe this book can take away some of your pain and replace it with laughter. No matter how hopeless a situation looks there is always hope. Hope can move a mountain and I hope that if these jokes make someone laugh, then I have truly served my purpose. So sit back, read, and enjoy. Welcome to Iky's world. I will make this guarantee to you readers. If you feel that this isn't a funny joke book, just send the book back to Iky, and he will keep the book and your money, then the joke will be on you!

Randy Lee Cassatt

One day Iky was walking along the beach and he found a magic lamp. Iky picked up the lamp and began to rub it. Suddenly, a Genie came out and said, "I am the Genie of the lamp and I will grant you three wishes." Iky thought for almost five minutes and then said, "Genie, I only want one wish. I wish that I didn't have manic-depressive disorder." The Genie asked, "What! Are you crazy?"

Iky was talking to his oldest brother Ort. Ort asked, "Iky, how have you been doing?" Iky answered, "I haven't been feeling too good lately." Ort asked, "Why, what's the matter?" Iky answered, "My hemorrhoids have been acting up again." Ort said, "I'm sorry to hear that. I did not even know you had them. How long have your hemorrhoids been bothering you?" Iky answered, "Well, ever since they moved next door to me."

One night at work, Iky's supervisor Ole caught him sleeping. When Ole woke Iky up, he yelled, "Iky, what do you think you're doing?" Iky answered, "What does it look like I'm doing? I was looking for you." "How could you be looking for me when you were sitting there snoring louder than a freight train?" yelled Ole. "I was trying to find you in my sleep, and by the way, is it lunch time yet? I sure would hate to sleep through my lunch break," answered Iky.

Iky was talking to his brother Bigfoot and Bigfoot said, "Bill Clinton and George Bush got into a big fight recently. The Secret Service men had to break it up." Iky asked, "I wonder if Hillary knows that Bill is still beating around the bush?"

Iky suffers from manic-depressive disorder. While he was having a session with his psychiatrist, Iky asked, "Hey Doc, am I really crazy?" The psychiatrist answered, "Well, let's find out. Give me three hundred dollars right now." Iky reached into his wallet and handed him the cash. The psychiatrist said, "Yes, you are definitely crazy." Iky asked, "How do you figure that?" His psychiatrist answered, "Because I usually get one hundred dollars a session."

Iky was born with major hearing loss. The best way to describe Iky's hearing - he is deaf in one ear and cannot hear out of the other. One day Iky got a phone call. A man said, "Hi there, my name is Mac Davis. I work for the Deaf and Hearing Impaired Charity Benefit Fund. Would you like to give a donation?" Iky said, "What?" After trying to talk to Iky for ten minutes, Mac sent Iky a donation.

Iky's neighbor Ralph stopped over to see him. When Ralph pulled into Iky's yard, he noticed an unfamiliar truck parked in the yard. Ralph asked, "Whose truck is that?" Iky answered, "That is Bigfoot's truck. He is one of my brothers." Ralph asked, "Well, where is Bigfoot right now?" Iky answered, "He is down in the woods hunting squirrel."

They talked for about an hour and then Ralph went home. When he got home, his wife Willa asked, "Ralph, how is Iky doing?" Ralph answered, "I'm a little worried about him because he thinks that his brother is a Bigfoot that knows how to drive a truck and likes to hunt squirrel." Willa sat there thinking for a while and then she said to Ralph, "I have always wondered what kind of food a Bigfoot eats."

Sometime ago, Iky was talking to his Mom and he was telling her how his medications would occasionally irritate his stomach. They would give him severe attacks of diarrhea. Iky would have many hits and runs. At first, it hit him and then he had to run to the bathroom. His Mom told him to go to the store and buy a box of Depends.

Four days went by. Then one morning Iky's Mom looked out the window and she saw Iky pulling into her yard. She walked outside and met him halfway. Iky said, "Mom, I want to thank you for telling me about the Depends. They really work well and they sure are comfortable. I thought that they were going to be big and bulky, but I don't even think anybody noticed that I am wearing them." His Mom said, "Iky, I am really happy that you like them. However, you are supposed to wear them inside your pants, not outside!"

Iky's friend Killer said, "The Plant Manager, Carol Flatchest had a living bra and it died."

Iky always said, "The only difference between a lawyer and a thief is that the lawyer has a license."

One morning Ort and Bigfoot drove out to Iky's place. As they got out of the truck, Ort reached behind the seat and pulled out a ten-pound sledgehammer. They called it the Iky doorbell because that was the only way Iky could hear anybody knocking on his door. As usual, Ort pounded on the door for about three minutes and Iky finally opened the door. Ort said, "Hey Iky, we came out to see you." Iky looked at them and said, "Okay," After saying that, Iky stepped back into his house and closed the door.

One Sunday morning Ort went over and had coffee with his Mom. Ort said, "The other day Iky told me that the best four years he had in school were when he was in the first grade." Mom said, "No, if I remember right, that was kindergarten."

Iky's illness finally progressed to the point where his psychiatrist decided that isolating himself from society would be best for Iky. Iky sold everything he had and moved to Alaska. He bought land four hundred miles north of Fairbanks. A bush pilot had to fly Iky to and from his property. He spent the entire summer building his cabin. The day Iky finished his cabin there were snowflakes in the air. One day while he was sitting on his porch, Iky saw smoke off to the north and he thought it might be a forest fire. A few days later, a rough looking mountain man appeared at Iky's cabin.

The mountain man said, "Howdy there neighbor. That was smoke from my campfire that you might have seen three days ago. I was trying to signal you so I could invite you over to my place for a great big party. Since you did not respond, I would like to teach you how to send and read smoke signals. Anyway, back to the party. At my party there is going to be lots of live entertainment - music, singing, dancing, and eating. There is going to be lots of heavy drinking, and a whole bunch of wild sex. Then, when the party is over, there's going to be a great big fight." Iky said, "That sounds like a lot of fun. Who is going to be at this party?" The Mountain Man said, "Aw, it's just going to be you and me."

Where Iky used to work, one of his supervisor's nicknames was Ironbox. One day, Iky's friend Larry walked up to Ironbox and said, "I would like to take you home with me tonight." Ironbox told him, "I think I will call your wife and tell her what you just said," Larry said, "Go ahead and call her. I was planning on watching you two!"

When Iky was in Saudi Arabia, he went to a shop that rented camels. Iky said to the owner Omar, "I would like to rent that big ugly camel right there." Omar said, "That is my wife." Iky was so embarrassed he said, "Sir, I sincerely apologize. Can I rent a camel from that herd over there?" Omar said, "I accept your apology, but that herd over there is my family." Iky said, "I guess you really are all a bunch of camel jockeys."

Jimbob Blowme, the assistant Human Resources Director, was more then qualified for his job. When he was a regular worker out on the floor, (I need to rephrase that sentence, because nobody ever saw him do any work) he would take your break when it came time for him to relieve you.

When Iky was in grade school, Lips came up to him and said, "Iky come with me. I have something to show you." Two other kids tagged along and they all went into the bathroom. In one toilet, there was a foot and a half long turd which was about two inches round and it was green and purple. Iky said, "My Dad always says that if you don't take a good healthy shit in the morning, you're not worth a shit all day." Beef said, "Yeah, but whatever took that shit won't have to go for another week. Our herd of cows doesn't even shit that much." Lips said, "Hey Beef, it kind of looks like you." Beef told Lips, "Shut up you dumb bastard!"

Iky ran over and flushed the toilet while they were standing there laughing. The toilet began to overflow. Leroy saw it and shouted, "There she blows, its Moby's Dick!" The turd was sticking halfway out of the toilet and it looked like a torpedo. Iky said, "Let's get out of here!" They all ran out the door, and bumped right into Mr. Larson, one of their teachers. Mr. Larson asked, "Why are all you boys in such a big hurry?" Beef said, "Because Lips was using the toilet and his butt plug fell out. It clogged up the toilet." Mr. Larson decided to make Lips clean up the mess. Later that day, Iky told Lips, "That's just like that old World War II saying." Lips asked, "What are you talking about?" Iky answered, "Loose Lips Sinks Ships."

One day Iky went to the drug store to get a new prescription filled. The pharmacist Don said, "These pills will give you gas." Iky said, "I can't believe the price of gas these days. About how many gallons can I expect to get out of that bottle?"

Iky was talking to his Dad and said, "That darn Bigfoot! I cannot figure him out. Every time I stop over at his house, I ask him if he wants to go get something to eat. Bigfoot always says the same thing. He says he has already eaten. He doesn't eat by the clock; Bigfoot just eats when he gets hungry." Dad said, "So do animals."

Iky was standing in line at the post office and there was a woman ahead of him. She had a very large package that she was pushing with a dolly. Iky said, "Woman, you sure do have a big box." The woman turned around and slapped Iky. Iky said, "I'm sorry, I made a mistake. I was talking about your large package. You have a little box." Then the woman kissed Iky.

Iky made plans with his cousin Alex to take an ice-fishing trip up north to Alex's place in Rogers, North Dakota and spend two weeks ice fishing with him. When Iky's vacation finally arrived, he loaded up his gear and headed for North Dakota. After sixteen hours of driving, Iky pulled into Alex's yard and saw Alex walking out of his house.

Alex said, "Man, it's quite a surprise to see you Iky." Iky said, "Yeah, I've really been looking forward to this ice fishing trip." Alex said, "I'm really glad that you could make it, but there's only one problem." Iky said, "I'm glad there's only one problem, because I don't think I can handle two. What's the problem?"

Alex said, "This is the Fourth of July." Iky asked, "Are you saying the ice isn't thick enough yet?" Alex answered, "There is no ice on the lake, you moron." Iky asked, "Well, how about over in Minnesota or up in Canada?" Alex answered, "There is no ice anywhere." Iky stood there shaking his head. Then he looked at Alex and said, "Those scientists must be right." Alex asked, "What in the hell are you talking about?" Iky answered, "It's got to be global warming."

Iky's friend Greg went to the bank to cash his Social Security check. Later that day Greg's wife asked, "Did you cash that check today?" Greg decided to make his wife jealous so he said, "Yes I did, and I even showed the teller my chest." She said, "You should have dropped your pants, then you could have gotten Social Security Disability."

Back in Bigfoot's partying days he would go out quite a lot. One weekend he decided to go out looking for some hot babes so he took a shower. He didn't have any shampoo, so he used a bar of Irish Spring soap. After he had lathered up, the bar of soap disappeared. He didn't think anything about it, just figured it went down the drain. Bigfoot had long blond hair and he just shook it out without combing it. He went out bar hopping all night and he couldn't find any chicks interested in him. In fact, they all looked at him strangely and some even laughed. He wondered what in the hell was wrong. After drinking several more beers to drown his sorrow, Bigfoot had to go relieve himself. After he had finished taking a leak, he walked over to the sink and started washing his hands. When he looked up in the mirror, Bigfoot saw something green stuck in his hair. It was the bar of Irish Spring soap! There is an expression for that, "Soap on dope."

Pamerrhoid Nobrains thinks that tax evasion is where there are thumbtacks on the highway and you have to do some evasive driving to avoid them.

Years ago, the drive-in theaters were very popular. One Saturday night, Iky took his girlfriend out to see a movie. He drove in and found a parking spot. Iky rolled down his window, took the speaker off the pole, hooked it on the window, and rolled the window back up. After the movie was finally over, Iky took his girlfriend back to her house and then drove another ten miles to get to his house.

Iky pulled into his yard and turned his truck off. When he started to open the truck door, he finally noticed the speaker was still in the window. The speaker cord was still attached to the pole that was dragging about fifty pounds of concrete on it. Iky thought to himself, "I was wondering what that damn noise was. I thought it was coming from the radio."

Ort decided to take Iky to an Arkansas Razorback football game. Ort was a big hog fan and halfway into the game, an Arkansas player scored a touchdown. The whole stadium went hog-wild. There were six hogs (I mean hog fans) exactly in front of Iky. They most likely weighed three hundred fifty pounds each. Ort was jumping around in excitement and he yelled at Iky, "What do you think of those hogs?" Iky yelled back, "I think they need to lose some weight!"

One evening Billy Joe was running the palletizer at work. The palletizer machine stacks the finished boxes of the product on pallets. During the stacking process, the boxes come down the conveyor line. One box got jammed up in the machine, and everything stopped. Billy Joe walked up on the catwalk and reached out to grab the jammed box. While Billy Joe was pulling on the box, a guide bar jumped out of place and pinned his hand. He pulled hard and freed his hand noticing the bar had scraped skin off the top of his hand.

Billy Joe went to see the nurse Sandra, and she put peroxide and bandages on his cuts and scrapes. The safety director, George Pigman wanted to know exactly what had happened. George followed Billy Joe back to the palletizer. While the machine was still running, Billy Joe said, "I was reaching in here like this to pull out a jammed box." While Billy Joe was looking at George and telling him what had happened, the guide bar jumped out of place again and pinned his injured hand.

George grabbed Billy Joe's arm and helped him get it out. Billy Joe said, "That's exactly how it happened."

Bigfoot always said, "The truth does not lie."

Recently, Iky flagged down a Highway Patrolman. When the officer asked Iky, "What's a matter?" Iky answered, "I think a matter is somebody who lays down mats." The Officer said, "I will rephrase the question. What is your problem?" Iky answered, "Well I have manic-depression, high blood pressure, high cholesterol, and I'm over worked and under sexed." "That's enough! Why did you flag me down?" asked the Officer. Iky answered, "They just robbed me at that gas station over there about ten minutes ago." The Officer asked, "Did you get a good look at the robbers?" Iky answered "Well sir, I'm not really sure who's responsible." The Officer asked, "If you aren't sure who robbed you, then how do you know that you've been robbed?" Iky answered, "Well Officer, if you had seen what I had to pay for gas, you would call it robbery too. And by the way, I have hearing loss too."

Iky told his friend Psycho, "Money cannot buy you happiness or love." "Psycho laughed and said, "Yes it can." Iky asked, "How do you figure that?" Psycho answered, "It can if you're a prostitute or a gigolo."

Jerkbob East, the workplace bully, always gave Iky a hard time. One of Jerkbob's problems was that he had the same I.Q. as a retarded jellyfish. Jerkbob asked Iky that old southern question, "Do you know the difference between a Yankee and a Damn Yankee?" Iky just stood there waiting patiently. Jerkbob finished, "A Yankee is a Northerner who comes down south and then goes back north. A Damn Yankee is a Northerner who comes down south and stays."

Iky smirked, "That joke is about as old as a fart in the wind. I'm going to tell you something Jerkoff, I mean Jerkbob. I was born in North Dakota and raised in Minnesota. I lived up North for nineteen years and I have lived down South for twenty-three years. The way I see it, my right butt cheek is the north and my left butt cheek is the south, and if you don't like me, then you can just kiss me right down my Mason Dixon Line."

Iky had just bought a brand-new washer and dryer. One day, Iky's Mom stopped over for a surprise visit. When she walked into the house, she could hear a terrible noise coming from the utility room. Mom asked Iky, "What in the world is happening in the utility room?" Iky answered, "Well, I'm using my new washer and dryer." Mom asked, "What did you put in them?" Iky answered, "It's just my dishes."

When Iky was in high school, he was an amateur boxer. Iky went to Red Lake, Minnesota for a boxing fight at a big Indian reservation in Northern Minnesota. As Iky got into the ring, he was moving around, bobbing, weaving, and shadowboxing. The ring announcer started the show and said, "In the blue corner from Detroit Lakes, Minnesota is Iky Cassatt." The audience booed and threw beer cans into the ring. A few tomahawks were thrown too, but they just bounced off Iky's head.

The moment Iky took his robe off, the crowd realized he was standing in the ring stark ass naked. Before the fight, Iky had been so nervous that he forgot to put on his cup and trunks. However, the announcer was a quick thinker and he said, "Iky's nickname is Chief Running Bare." After that announcement, the whole audience stood up and cheered for Iky.

Jimbob Blowme thinks that D.V.D. stands for "Dangerous Venereal Disease!"

Iky put on his best clothes and took his girlfriend out on a big date. He wined and dined her, then took her back to his place. Right before they were going to make love Iky's girlfriend asked him, "Do you want to make love using a condom?" Iky answered, "Well no, I would rather make love to you."

Pamerrhoid Nobrains, the human resources director, almost choked to death on bubble gum. The problem solving team spent the next three days showing Nobrains how to open the bag of gum first.

Iky was having a manic episode when he called Bigfoot and said, "Hey Bigfoot, you are not going to believe what just happened to me!" Bigfoot said, "Well, tell me what happened." Iky said, "I walked down to the pond to feed the fish and a talking bullfrog hopped up to me. The bullfrog told me he would grant me three wishes." Bigfoot asked, "Did you get your three wishes?" Iky answered, "No, I did not." Bigfoot asked, "Why, what happened?" Iky answered, "The bullfrog croaked."

Iky decided to eat at the New Mexican restaurant in town. He walked into the restaurant and sat down at a table. He saw a large menu board hanging on the wall. The waiter walked up to his table and asked, "What would you like to order, Senor?" Iky said, "I'll take a large iced tea and the Alamo Surprise." The waiter yelled, "The Gringo wants the Alamo Surprise!"

Suddenly the kitchen door burst wide open. Fifteen Mexicans with ball bats and broomsticks ran straight to Iky's table. While they were whacking on Iky, they yelled, "Remember the Alamo!" This went on for about thirty seconds, and then the Mexicans ran back into the kitchen.

Iky was lying on the floor all battered and bruised. The waiter walked over to Iky, dumped a large iced tea over his head, and then asked Iky, "Would you like to have some refried beans and guacamole to go with that, Davey Crockett? Better yet, just come back tomorrow! Tomorrow's surprise is Montezuma's Revenge!"

Iky said, "Jerkbob East is so fat that whenever he goes to Mount Rushmore, the tourists always ask the Park Ranger the same question - "Which president is that?"

Iky went to get the Union Shop Steward Harvey to go with him to see the plant manager, Carol Flatchest. Iky had concerns that needed to be resolved before his shift was over. As they were walking to Flatchest's office, they saw her door was wide open and she was in the middle of the room doing a picture perfect headstand. Flatchest's head was on the floor and her feet were sticking straight up in the air. Iky looked at Harvey and asked, "What in the world is she doing?" Harvey answered, "Well, when you're a plant manager, sometimes you just have to use your head."

Iky was talking to his friend Psycho and he asked, "Have you ever seen that movie Cliffhanger?" Psycho said, "No I haven't seen that movie. What is it about?" Iky answered, "John Lithgow plays an evil villain." Psycho looked surprised and asked, "What other kind of villain is there?"

Iky's first boxing fight was a total disappointment. While he was in the middle of the second round, Iky was disqualified. Jim, Iky's coach said, "Iky, don't worry about this fight. Just make sure from now on, fight during the three minute fight round and rest during the one minute rest period." Iky said, "The reason I did what I did was because after fighting the first round I needed a three minute rest."

Iky got addicted to gambling at the casinos. Iky's Mom asked him one day, "Iky, how many days have you been to the casino this week?" Iky answered, "Every day." Mom asked, "Do you have a gambling problem?" Iky answered, "Yes I do, because I haven't been winning."

Iky and his friend A.J. were in the cafeteria having a hypothetical conversation about religion. A.J. said, "Religion is like a plant. First, you start with a seed. You plant the seed in the ground and water it. As the seed germinates and starts to grow, you fertilize it and pull the weeds out around it because they take the nutrients away from your plant. Sometimes you prune it to make the plant stronger. It has to have plenty of sunlight, and over time, you have a mature healthy plant. This is the same with religion."

Iky said, "Do you know what happens to you when your plant is fully matured?" A.J. asked, "No, what happens?" Iky answered, "The D.E.A. flies over your house with a helicopter and they see your plant. Then they drive to your house and pull your plant up. The D.E.A. takes you to jail, takes your picture, and finger prints you. Then you get to be an instant celebrity in the community, because you're on the local ten o-clock news and in the newspapers as well. You receive a four thousand dollar fine and five hundred dollars court costs. You become a felon, and then on top of that, you lose your job. That's not including your lawyers' fees. That's what happened to Maryjane Hemply." A.J. laughingly said, "Next time grow a tomato plant, not the forbidden fruit!"

Iky's brother Ort is a building contractor for Beast-Ears Construction. One day while he was working at a construction site, the O.S.H.A. (Occupational Safety and Health Administration) man showed up. Ort called them 'Overpaid Scum and Heartless Administration.' He didn't like the man because he was always looking for safety violations. Ort knew that several workers were using a twelve-foot ladder to get on the roof of the building on which they were working. They were also stepping on the top step of the ladder, which is considered a safety violation.

After the O.S.H.A. man made his way around the job site, he went and got Ort. The O.S.H.A. man said, "I have a problem that needs to be addressed whenever possible." Ort followed the O.S.H.A. man over to the ladder. The O.S.H.A. man said, "I want to talk to the workers that are up on the roof. Can you please call them down for me?" Ort started yelling at the workers but they didn't hear him because of the noisy air tools. Ort climbed up three steps on the ladder and started yelling again. They still didn't hear him. Ort was getting very angry at this point. He climbed about half way up the ladder, started yelling again, and still, they didn't hear him. Finally, Ort completely lost his mind, climbed to the very top of the ladder and stood on top of it screaming his lungs out.

The next morning Ort had to report to the main office. His boss showed him a picture the O.S.H.A. man had taken the day before. It showed Ort standing on top of a twelve-foot ladder with his mouth wide open and his face was beet red. Ort got a horrendous butt chewing and the construction company got a thousand-dollar fine. When Iky found out what happened, he called Ort and said, "That reminds me of that old saying." Ort asked, "What are you talking about?" Iky answered, "A picture is worth a thousand dollars." Ort said, "Iky, that is supposed to be a picture is worth a thousand words." Iky said, "Yeah, but I know how you are. You said a thousand cuss words that cost you a thousand dollars!"

Bigfoot asked Mike, "What does the starship enterprise and toilet paper have in common?" Mike answered, "Both have boldly gone where no man has gone before." Bigfoot laughed and said, "I like your punch line better than mine. Mine was both circle your anus in search of klingons."

ky has a large bald spot on top of his head – when you come right down to it, on his whole head. While Iky was in the cafeteria at work, Jerkbob East walked up to Iky and said, "Hey bonehead, the south is going to rise and do it again." Iky said, "Listen Jerkoff." Jerkbob said, "That's Jerkbob." Iky said, "That's what I said. Do you know how high the south will rise this time?" Jerkbob asked, "No, how high?" Iky answered, "High enough to kiss a damn Yankee's ass."

<u>Management People Are So Dumb That:</u>

1. They move to a different state whenever there is a time change.

2. They think that Band-Aid is a charity benefit for band members who have aids.

3. They think that Downtime is when someone trips and falls down.

4. They think that Uptime is when someone picks himself or herself up after they have fallen.

5. They have to look at family pictures in the offices to see if they are in the right office.

6. They answer a question with a question.

7. They come out of the restroom with a butt gasket around their neck and say, "Look at my new neck tie."

8. They think that overtime is employees who need to be retired.

9. They think that a rubber band is an orchestra that plays rubber instruments.

10. 10. They cannot figure out why there is always one person missing at the meetings.

Iky walked into the bank to get a loan. The Loan Officer asked Iky, "What do you have for collateral?" Iky asked, "What's that?" The Loan Officer said, "Well, do you have a house, property, car, checking account, or a job?" Iky answered, "If I had all of that I wouldn't need a loan."

Bigfoot is so cheap that in order to keep his electric bill down he charges his cell phone in his truck.

Iky always kept his medication in a small cooking pot that he put into a beer cooler. One morning he couldn't find the beer cooler and he was getting late for work. He decided to leave without his medications. He got into his truck and headed to work. After he traveled about four or five miles, Iky decided that he better go back and try to find his medication. Iky turned his truck around and took off like a bat out of hell.

A state trooper pulled him over for speeding. The Officer said, "I would like to see your driver's license." Iky handed him his fishing license. The Officer said, "This is not your driver's license, you gave me your fishing license, and why do you have a fishing line and a hook dragging behind your bumper?" Iky answered, "Because I am trolling." The Officer said, "Your tags are expired." Iky handed him a hunting license and said, "I bought the tags yesterday." The Officer asked, "Are you hunting right now too?" Iky answered, "No sir, I only do that at night."

The Officer asked, "Are you on alcohol or drugs?" Iky answered, "No Sir." "Then why were you speeding back there?" asked the Officer. Iky answered, "Sir, I'm in a hurry because I'm late for work. I need my drugs, and I can't find my beer cooler or my pot." "Are you crazy?" asked the Officer. Iky answered, "You should ask my psychiatrist that question. But it will cost you three hundred dollars.

Nobrains was telling Flatchest at a meeting, "Silence is Golden." Flatchest said, "Then, shut up!"

Iky was talking to his neighbor Ralph about the bible. Ralph said, "Euthanasia is a moral sin." Iky said, "I didn't know that it was a sin to be youth in Asia. I guess they must be Communist." Ralph said, "No Iky, I said euthanasia." Iky said, "I heard you the first time, youth in Asia." Ralph said, "Euthanasia is when people perform mercy killings." Iky said, "Now I understand. It is like the time when those Chinese students were protesting, and their government sent in the Army. The Army massacred thousands of their youth in Asia, but I don't think that was mercy killing."

The company put a new cereal production manager named Asshwipe Schmidt over the label line department for two weeks. Production fell by twenty-five percent. Asshwipe wrote himself up since he had made such an ass wipe out of himself.

Iky was standing in line at the bank. A customer behind him saw that Iky had a Disability Check. The man asked, "What's the difference between your Social Security Disability Check and my Social Security

Check?" Iky said, "Let me see your check." The man handed Iky his check. Iky looked the check over, handed it back to him, and said, "About six hundred dollars."

One night at work, Iky went out to the smoking patio. At that time, Iky was smoking O.P.C. cigarettes. O.P.C stands for 'other people's cigarettes.' Dominico was standing out on the patio smoking a cigarette with his back against the railing. Iky walked up to him and said, "Hey Dominico, give me a cigarette." Dominico didn't say a word. He just stood there with a lit cigarette hanging out of the corner of his mouth with a stupid blank stare on his face. Iky thought he might not have heard him so Iky said again, "Dominico, give me a cigarette." There still was no response from him.

Iky said, "What is your problem? Give me a darn cigarette!" To the right side of Iky, there was a group of smokers laughing. Iky said, "Give me a gosh darn cigarette!" Dominico still had that stupid blank looking stare on his face. Iky said, "Dominico this is what I think of you." Iky raised his right leg and he cut loose with a thunder booming fart. Everybody out there was laughing except Dominico.

Iky started to notice that they continued laughing. Iky thought that something wasn't right, so he turned around. There was a woman sitting behind him that he had never seen before. As Iky began to melt with embarrassment, the woman slapped her leg, laughed and said, "Aw, don't worry about it! I have five brothers who act just like you!" Dominico burst out laughing, and handed Iky a cigarette. From then on, Iky bought his own cigarettes.

Ort, Iky's brother, recently had a big family gathering at his house. Ort's wife, Ellymae Junebug Campatt, had invited all of her southern relatives. Out on their patio were tables and chairs set up for all the guests. Iky had his back against the railing smoking a cigarette. The day before, Iky had shaved off his long beard that he had been growing for the last five years. Ellymae was busy setting the food out on the tables. As she glanced up, she saw Iky and for a moment, she thought Iky was her husband Ort. Then she realized that it was Iky. She said, "Iky, for a minute I thought you were Ort." Iky said, "Don't worry Ellymae; I won't climb in bed with you." Billyjoe Jeffbob, Ellymae's son laughed and said, "Ort won't even get in bed with her anymore because she snores too loud."

Iky's nephew Cave Man said, "Hey Uncle Ike, I got tickets to the Metallica Concert and I even got a pass into the Mosh Pit." Iky asked, "What's that? Is it like a snake pit?" Cave Man answered, "No man, the Mosh Pit is a lowered section of the floor in front of the band and the people who are in the pit act wild, crazy, hysterical, and stupid. They do dumb things like pick people up over their heads and pass them around to other people in the crowd." Iky said, "That sounds just like the Ayatollah Khomeini's funeral."

Ort, Bigfoot, and Iky were discussing former presidents. Ort said, "I like Franklin Delano Roosevelt because he said, "The only thing you have to fear is fear itself." Bigfoot said, "I like John Fitzgerald Kennedy because he said, "Ask not what your country can do for you, but what you can do for your country.'" Iky said, "I like what William Jefferson Clinton said. He said, "I did not have sex with that woman!"

Ort said, "Clinton was a liar because he later admitted he had an affair with Monica Lewinsky, and the man was under oath when he lied." Bigfoot said, "A president is supposed to set a good example for the country and the world. They should have impeached Clinton for pulling that stunt." Iky said, "F.D.R and J.F.K were both having affairs with other women and they have proven that. Bill did set an example although it was a bad one and he wasn't lying when he said, "I did not have sex with that woman." He was talking about his wife Hillary!"

Roger's friend Jake worked at a battery factory. A worker quit and the personnel department didn't hire anyone to replace him. It was the middle of summer, and Jake's supervisor was working him to death. One day the secretary ran into the supervisor's office and shouted, "You need to get out there on the floor and see what Jake is doing!"

Jack, the supervisor, walked out on the floor and saw Jake. Jake was pushing one cart and pulling another one that was full of batteries.

Jake's clothes were dripping wet with sweat, his fly was unzipped, and his snake was hanging out. Jack ran up to him and shouted, "Have you lost your mind? What in the world do you think you're doing?" Jake answered, "Well, you're not hiring anybody to help me and I'm tired of you jacking me around. If you're going to make me work like a mule, than I'm going to look and act like one."

Iky said, "If you listen really close whenever a brown-noser sneezes, you can hear them say, "Aw, shit." Then they wipe there butt with toilet paper.

Iky can't figure out the lazy jocks at work. (A jock is a nobody who thinks they are a has been.) They get paid to do their job and then they will not do it. Then they go down to the gym after work and pay money to work out. Dumb!

When Iky was a little boy, he went with his parents, brothers, and sister to one of their friend's house. The couple also had children. While there, Iky found a toy that when squeezed, made a high-pitched squeaking noise. Iky placed the toy up against his ear and squeezed it with all his might. Then he ran around the house screaming, "I can't hear!" Several days later Bigfoot composed a song for Iky, and this is how it went:

> "Who can squeak a way up high?"
> "Iky spit in his eye,"
> "Everyone knows its Squeaky,"
> "Who squeaked in Iky's ear?"
> "Iky don't think he can hear."

Nobrains thinks that Copenhagen chewing tobacco comes from Denmark.

Psycho told Iky about his friend named Steve who was in the Coast Guard. Steve was flown to a remote island in the Pacific Ocean. Steve asked some sailors already there, "What do you do for entertainment here?" They told him, "Friday nights we drive to the bar on the other side of the island and we get shit faced drunk until we all pass out."

Steve said, "Well, I don't really like to get that drunk." Then they said, "Saturday nights we go to the whore house on the other side of the island and we hump whores all night long." Steve said, "I really don't care for that either." They asked Steve, "Are you gay?" Steve said, "No, I'm not." They laughed and said, "Well then, Sunday nights you definitely don't want to go anywhere on the other side of the island!"

Iky was talking to Ort and he asked, "Did you hear about Bigfoot's big date that he had the other night?" Ort asked, "No I didn't hear anything about it. What happened?" Iky answered, "Nothing."

Many years ago little Iky and his Mom and Dad took a cross-country trip. While they were driving by a cemetery, Iky asked, "I wonder how many people are dead in there?" Mom answered, "All of them." As they passed a large state penitentiary, Iky asked, "What's that building?" Dad answered, "That's where most of the murderers, robbers, rapists, child molesters, psychos, thieves, pimps, and dope heads are at. It's the scum of society." Iky said, "I've always wondered where that capital building was." Dad said, "That's my boy."

When Bigfoot was growing up at home, one Christmas he got a toy bowling ball set. He took two of the bowling balls, put them under his shirt, and had them sticking out on his chest. It was his impersonation of Dolly Pardon. While Dad was sitting in his recliner watching television, Bigfoot walked into the living room showing off his new boob job. When Dad saw him, he yelled, "I never want to see that again!" A little while later Iky walked into the living room. Dad saw Iky and said, "Now, that looks better." Iky had a bowling pin sticking out of his pant's zipper! That was Iky's impersonation of John Holmes. It's just like that saying, "Walk like a man, not like a woman."

Iky was talking to his Mom on the phone and she asked him, "How did your appointment with the psychiatrist go yesterday? Iky answered, "Well, when I walked into the building, I got into the elevator and went up four floors. The elevator raised my outlook on life. Then I realized I had left my insurance papers in my truck. When I took the elevator back down, it lowered my outlook on life, and I became very depressed." With great concern Iky's Mom asked him, "Well, what did your psychiatrist do?" Iky replied, "Aw, it was simple. He prescribed me Prozac and told me to stay out of elevators."

Iky has a great big bald spot on his head; the best way to describe his head is it looks like a giant dodo bird's nest with one big egg in the middle. Dodo birds are extinct, and so is Iky's hair. Iky was over at Bigfoot's place and they were watching television. A commercial came on advertising hair restoration treatment. They were showing pictures of bald men before the treatment, and pictures of men with full heads of hair after the treatment. Iky said, "I'll bet that stuff wouldn't have helped Custer." Bigfoot said, "I'll bet that stuff wouldn't help you."

Carol Flatchest, the plant manager, doesn't have any boobs. Senior citizens at the local nursing home used her as a shuffleboard table on weekends. Iky's friend Meano walked up to her one day and said, "Carol, I'm going to tell you a joke that's so funny, it will make you laugh so hard your boobs will fall off." Meano stood there looking at her chest for a minute and then stated, "Oh, I see you must have heard that joke already."

Iky says, "Seniority at work doesn't mean anything if you don't have it."

Bigfoot and Iky were driving down the road; Bigfoot had just taken a drink from his soda. Then Iky grabbed the soda, and he threw it out the window. Bigfoot said in anger, "What did you do that for?" Iky asked, "Didn't you see that sign back there?" Bigfoot asked, "What sign?" Iky said, "The sign that read, 'Do not drink and drive!'"

Iky's first wife Death had been around the block many times over, and she was still going around the block. When she was married to Iky, just out of curiosity Iky asked her, "How many guys have you slept with?" Death answered, "Well, the last time I figured it up it was right at fifty thousand." Iky yelled, "What did you do, sleep with Wilt Chamberlain too? Did you hire an accountant to figure it up for you?" Death answered, "Oh, I forgot it is fifty thousand two and we weren't sleeping!"

Iky does not do illegal drugs because he is messed up enough already. Iky takes legal drugs that are affordable, like beer and whiskey.

Iky has two friends, Jake and Moe who do many drugs every chance they get. Well, one day when Jake and Moe were going to smoke some marijuana, they took an empty coke can and pressed a dent into the can's side. They poked a small hole in the can where the dent was, and then put some marijuana in the dent over the hole. Moe was holding the can sideways, and Jake fired it up for him. Moe started inhaling out of the can's opening, and he took too big of a hit. He was gagging, coughing, and almost throwing up. Iky said, "I knew that you guys shouldn't have been mixing coke with pot."

Ort, Bigfoot, and Iky were over at their Mom's house watching the Discovery Channel. The program they were watching was about the Earth's oceans. Ort said, "That's really amazing how the moon causes the tides here on Earth." Iky said, "It's the gravitational pull of the moon gases that causes the tides." Bigfoot said, "Iky, you idiot! There are no gases on the moon." Iky said, "Well, it must be true." Ort asked, "What are you talking about Iky?" Iky answers, "Those Russians must have beaten us to it."

Iky went to the hardware store and bought an electric weed eater. One Friday his Mom asked him, "Iky, can you come over this weekend and weed eat my yard for me?" Iky said, "Sure Mom, but only if you buy thirty-five miles of electric cord!" Mom said, "I have a ten-foot electric cord."

Iky bought property in the Boston Mountains in Arkansas. His brothers and friends helped him build his house. Iky lived so far out in the boonies sunlight had to be pumped in! While Iky was at work, Jerkbob East and his sidekick Jimbob Blowme started giving Iky a hard time. Jimbob Blowme had the I.Q. of a scrambled egg because he thought that a chicken would hatch out of an eggplant.

Jerkbob said, "We heard that you live up in the mountains Iky. I guess now you think you're a hillbilly." Jimbob slyly said, "Yeah, we know what goes on up in those mountains, don't we Jerkbob? Iky makes love to his goats, pigs and sheep." Iky said, "You forgot my chickens too." The inbreeds, Jerkbob and Jimbob were standing there laughing. Iky told them, "You know, just because that is part of your culture, don't think it's a part of mine. That's the difference between you and me. I like to make love to women not animals. So you can just Blowme, Jimbob."

Brown-nosers say, "Once you get past the smell you got it licked." I think that is how that saying goes!

One night Bigfoot and Iky were doing some heavy drinking – in other words, they weren't drinking light beer. Bigfoot said, "I almost forgot to tell you that you're supposed to call Mom, Iky." Iky said, "I would rather call Mom, Mom, Bigfoot." Bigfoot said, "I don't think that Mom wants to be called Mom, Mom, Bigfoot." Iky asked, "Where are we at?" Bigfoot answered, "I don't know Iky." Iky said, "Then next time, I will have Mom introduce us."

Psycho said to Iky, "Jerkbob East is so fat that whenever he takes a bath he uses half a cup of water, and five gallons spill over out of the tub." Iky said, "They call that a hangover."

Iky was talking to his friend Meano, who is from Missouri. Iky asked him, "Have you ever noticed that whenever you talk to someone from Arkansas, eighty percent of the time they say that they are from a different state if you ask them where they are from? I wonder why that is?" Meano answered, "That's because years ago they outlawed brother and sister marriages." Iky thought for a while and said, "When they pass the next law that outlaws parents from marrying their children, there won't be any Arkies left in Arkansas."

One winter Iky went ice fishing with his Uncle Gus and Cousin Shannon in Bismarck North Dakota. Iky's Uncle Gus is a full-blooded German, and considered himself a professional beer drinker because he drinks lots of German beer. Cousin Shannon is a professional angler. Gus and Shannon decided they would pull an old northern joke on Iky. They went out on the frozen lake and Gus drilled several large holes in the thick layer of ice with his ice auger. He handed Iky a baseball bat and an opened can of peas.

Shannon said, "Iky, I want you to sit on that bucket, take a handful of the peas and put them all around each hole. Be ready with the baseball bat because when a fish comes up to take a pea, you club them on the head. After you have knocked them out, just throw them off to the side. We're going fishing about a mile from here, and we'll be back in two hours."

As they got into their truck, they were laughing while they drove to the other side of the lake. After two hours had gone by, they went back to check on Iky. Gus and Shannon were very aggravated, because they didn't even have a bite. As they were driving up to Iky, they saw that there were many fish lying around every hole. Iky saw them and yelled, "Hey guys, I ran out of peas an hour ago! And, you will never guess what else. Toilet paper works too! Do you have an extra baseball bat? I just broke that one, and I'm really knocking the shit out of these fish."

Carol Flatchest thinks that Lobsters are fat gangsters.

One day Iky was out in his yard and he was in the midst of a manic episode. Iky had put a dog collar around a dogwood tree. While he was hooking the leash on the collar, his neighbor Goosie came driving up. Goosie asked, "What are you doing Iky?" Iky answered, "I just got this new dog and I'm going to take him for a walk." Goosie said, "That sure looks like a bad vicious dog to me." Iky said, "Aw, he's not so bad. His bark is much worse than his bite!"

Iky walked into Al's Barber Shop and sat down in the barber-chair. Al looked at Iky and asked, "Well, what do you want, a cup of coffee or do you want to read a book?" Iky said, "I would like to get my hair cut." Al asked, "Well, which hair - your ear hair or your nose hair? If you want, I can even shave your arm pits." Iky said, "I would like the hair on my head cut!" Al said, "There is only one and a half hairs there, I am not a miracle worker; what do you want me to do?" Iky said, "Shave them off."

Al walked over to his desk, opened a drawer, and got out a roll of duct tape. He tore off a piece of the tape, stuck it on Iky's head, and then pulled it off. Iky stood up and looked into the big mirror hanging on the wall. Iky said, "Al, that's the best looking hair cut I have ever had. How much do I owe you?" Al reached into his wallet and handed Iky a hundred-dollar bill. Al yelled, "Now get the hell out of here and don't ever come back again!"

Iky's hunting friend Joey is from Alabama so Iky called him Alabama. Alabama only had two things on his mind; one was deer hunting and the other was his hunting hat. Alabama asked Iky, "What's the difference between beer nuts and deer nuts?" Iky answered, "I don't know - about three pounds?" Alabama said, "Try again" Iky said, "Well, I suppose beer nuts taste better." Alabama said, "I think I'm going to give up deer hunting and just sit around and eat beer nuts." Iky said, "I guess you got burned out on deer nuts huh?"

Alabama said, "Iky, you remind of a squirrel because he just sits there and chews on his nuts." Iky asked, "You mean acorns? By the way, what is the difference between beer nuts and deer nuts?" Alabama answered, "About thirty-five miles! I'm going to have to tell you this punch line, because I'm not going to stay out in these woods all night Iky. The difference between beer nuts and deer nuts is beer nuts are a buck twenty nine, and deer nuts are under a buck."

When Iky was cashing his check at the bank, the teller asked, "How would you like to have your check cashed? One large bill with several small bills, or do you want them all to be small bills?" Iky got so confused he said, "I'll just take a check."

The last year that Iky lived in Minnesota, one weekend he was home in bed sick. The phone rang so he got up and answered it, "Hello?" "Hey Iky, this is Bruce. What are you doing man? You're missing my big party, and everybody is wondering where you're at. The house and garage is full of people." Iky said, "Bruce, I'm not feeling good right now." Bruce asked, "Are you all right? What is the matter man?" Iky answered, "I got a really bad case of diarrhea." Bruce said, "Well hell, bring it along! These Norwegians, Finlanders and Polacks will drink anything!"

Iky thinks that the Green Bay Packers are triple X movie stars.

While Iky was in a Casino playing one of the slot machines, a woman sitting next to him said, "I'm really getting sick of these casinos. Every time I drop a hundred dollars into one of these machines, I never get anything back!" Iky said, "I know how you can get some money back." The woman asked, "Well, what is your secret?" Iky answered, "Give me a hundred dollars and I'll show you." The woman gave Iky a hundred dollars. Iky gave her ten dollars back and said, "There you go; now you got some money back. Do you want to try that again?"

Iky's first wife Death would have driven any normal man crazy, but her tactics did not affect Iky, because he was already crazy. Whenever they would make love, Death would make Iky wear a blindfold. One day Death was yelling at Iky but not because he was deaf. "I'm going to make your life a living hell!" she yelled. Iky said, "What are you going to do to me this time? Take my blindfold away from me and start walking around the house naked? I'll bet the window peeper doesn't have to wear a blindfold." Death yelled, "He's one of my regular costumers!" Iky said, "Yeah, and what am I – unleaded?"

Iky gets paranoid at times - he thinks everything is a conspiracy. He won't lick envelopes because he believes that currently all somebody has to do to frame you is get a sample of your D.N.A. from your saliva on an envelope. Iky had a brainstorm and now his dog Brownie licks all of his envelopes!

When gas was almost four dollars a gallon Iky was talking to his neighbor Ralph about it. Iky said, "This gas situation is getting out of hand. I have always paid cash for everything. I don't believe in credit cards and I have never had one. However, now I might have to get one just so I can pay for gas if I don't have enough cash." Ralph said, "You ought to get one of those Oklahoma Gas Credit Cards." Iky asked, "What's that?" Ralph answered, "It's a rubber hose about three and a half feet long." Iky said, "I'm going over to Oklahoma right now and get one!"

Iky, Psycho, and Tommy were the crew that cleaned up the Meat stick Room at their old job. Their supervisor at that time was Ironbox, and she was quite a character. Iron Box rules her department not with an iron fist but with an iron dildo, at times she would sit in her office arguing with herself most of the time. Once she even wrote herself up, because she couldn't agree with herself. She decided to call the clean up crew into her office for a butt-chewing meeting.

Ironbox said, "We have a very serious problem in the Meat stick Room." Tommy said, "We don't have a problem, because at least we know where the room is." Psycho said, "We have noticed a problem ever since you took over this department." Iky said, "I have a problem, because I can't get my time card to work in the A.T.M. machine."

Ironbox said, "Last night the U.S.D.A. (United States Department of Agriculture) Inspector wrote us up again. He found a couple of spray bottles in the room that didn't have labels on them. There was green stuff in one bottle and red stuff in the other." Psycho said "So what!" Ironbox yelled, "Those bottles need to have labels on them!"

Iky said, "Anybody who has ever worked clean up knows that green stuff is Solvent and red stuff is Servac Acid." Ironbox yelled, "I don't care what they are! Just put labels on the bottles that specify what's in them!" The clean up crew went back to the Meat stick Room. They made two labels and put them on the bottles. The labels read, "This Is Green Stuff" and "This Is Red Stuff."

One evening Iky stopped over to see his friend George. While they were in the living room drinking a few beers. Iky noticed a small square box on the fireplace mantle. Iky asked, "George, what's in that box?" George answered, "Aw it's just my Dad's ashes because they cremated him." Iky said, "He looks like he's lost a lot of weight."

The factory where Iky worked was so noisy that everybody had to wear earplugs. One morning when Iky was out on the floor working, Jerkbob East was trying to tell Iky something. Iky couldn't hear anything that he was saying. Therefore, Jerkbob got right in Iky's face and yelled at the top of his lungs. Iky got a whiff of Jerkbob's breath, and it was bad enough to gag a sewer worker wearing two gas masks!

After work, Iky stopped at a grocery store and bought Jerkbob a big breath mint. The next morning Iky gave it to him, and Jerkbob sucked on it all day long. When their shift was over, Jerkbob walked up to Iky and said, "Thank you for that big breath mint Iky. By the way, what was that thing called?" Iky said, "2001Flushes."

Boris said, "Women are like fish in a pond. If you catch something you don't like, you can always throw it back!"

Iky and Death were having a conversation and he was finally able to get in a few words, only because she had run out of wind. Iky said, "My cousin Alex told me the difference between a northern girl and a southern girl." Death said, "Everybody knows that a northern girl is from the North and a southern girl is from the South!"

Iky said, "I'm amazed that you could figure that one out. I thought that you were going to have to call up your boyfriend and have him help you with that one. Oh, I forgot that your uncle is having lunch right now. The difference between a northern girl and southern girl is, a northern girl says, "Yes, you can," and a southern girl says, "Yes, you all can!" Death said, "That just shows you that northern girls don't know how to have fun." Iky answered, "That just shows you that ever since I married you, I should have stayed up north!"

Killer says, "Management is the next best thing to Ex-Lax."

Carol Flatchest thinks that second-hand smoke is a person who has a cigarette in both hands.

Meano said to Iky, "Jerkbob East is so fat that whenever he takes a shower the water never reaches his feet, because it evaporates by the time it reaches his ankles!" Iky, said, "Well at least he doesn't have to worry about slipping on a bar of soap."

Many years ago, Iky went duck hunting with his Dad. They had just finished setting out all of the duck decoys, and as they were waiting behind the blind, a large flock of ducks began to land. Iky's Dad whispered, "Use your duck call Iky." Iky couldn't hear so he asked, "What did you say, Dad?" Dad said louder, "Use your duck call Iky!" Iky asked, "Did you say them ducks are small?" Then Iky's Dad lost it and shouted, "USE YOUR DAMN DUCK CALL IKY!" Iky said, "Quit yelling Dad! You just scared those ducks away!"

Iky was in a tough boxing fight. His opponent threw a vicious barrage of punches that knocked Iky through the ropes. His head hit the bell at the timekeeper's table and made a loud dinging noise. As Iky was lying on the floor knocked out, two spectators were watching him. One of the spectators said to the other, "Who is that guy?" The other spectator said, "I don't know, but his face sure rings a bell."

Iky's psychiatrist had given him some new prescriptions, so he went to the local drug store to get them filled. The pharmacist Don told Iky, "These medications have a lot of bad side effects." Iky asked, "What kind of side effects are you talking about?" Don began to explain the side effects in detail. "This green pill will give you gas, the orange one will give you indigestion, the blue one will give you upset stomach, and the white one will give you diarrhea." Upon hearing this, Iky turned around and started walking out the door. Don yelled, "Hey Iky, what about your medications?" Iky said, "Forget it Don, I'll just go and get a bottle of Pepto Bismol; it's cheaper."

Pamerrhoid Nobrains thinks, "That is impossible."

Benny asked Iky, "What separates the Okies from the Polacks?" Iky thought for a while and said, "The Atlantic Ocean?" Benny said, "Well Iky, you're almost right! Actually it's the Arkansas River." Iky said, "I didn't know the Arkansas River was in Poland!"

Iky decided to eat at a Kentucky Fried Chicken restaurant. The woman behind the counter asked Iky, "Would you like to try some of our buffalo wings?" Iky said, "That is really amazing how far they have come with that stem cell research program! But how do they catch those flying buffalos?"

Iky was walking along the beach, and he stubbed his toe on a shiny lamp. Iky picked up the lamp and rubbed the sand off it. A Genie came out of the lamp and told Iky, "I will grant you three wishes." Iky said, "You aren't real, you're just a figment of my imagination." The Genie said, "I will show you that I am real. I have just made you crap in your pants."

Iky stood there laughing at the Genie. The Genie asked him, "What is so funny?" Iky answered, "This reminds me of the diarrhea song, and I will sing it for you, 'Diarrhea cha cha cha diarrhea cha cha cha, some people think it's funny but it's really dark and runny.' I don't need a Genie to make me crap in my pants. I already had crap in my pants before I found you and your damn lamp because I have diarrhea." Iky dropped the lamp and walked away.

Iky and his Mom were shopping for some clothes. Iky found a pair of pants that he really liked. He went into the dressing room and tried them on. Then he came out to show his Mom. Iky said, "I really like these old style pants. I like this trap door in the back but thought they quit making these pants years ago." Iky's Mom looked at him and said, "Iky, you have put the pants on backwards."

While Bigfoot was working on his truck he said, "Iky, I need a socket." Iky punched Bigfoot in the arm. Bigfoot said, "Iky, I need a crescent wrench." Iky went to the house and brought back a crescent roll. Bigfoot said, "Iky, I need a Bud Light." Iky went to town, came back and he handed it to Bigfoot. Bigfoot yelled, "I said a Bud Light, not a Butt Light!"

Iky's Uncle Tom told him that every year when he was in college they would have a Gong Show. For all you who don't know what a Gong Show is – it's a show where people put on a performance on stage in front of a crowd of people. Three judges decided whether they liked or disliked the acts. If they didn't like an act, they stood up, hit a big gong, and then the show was over. If an act went all the way to the end without being gonged, the judges rated the act on a scale from one to ten. The winner got a trophy and prize money.

Tom said, "I had this college buddy named Evan. Evan paid the entry fee and signed up for the Gong Show. He told everybody that he was going to win the show, and on the night of the show, the whole auditorium was packed. Halfway into the show Evan went behind the stage. When it was Evan's turn, the announcer said, "And for our last and final act, Evan will give his impersonation of Tarzan the Ape Man coming home after a hard day's work." The curtain rises and suddenly you hear, "Ah Ahaaa Ahaaa!" Evan came swinging out on a rope, totally butt naked, and he was puking, pissing and shitting at the same time. Everybody was laughing there asses off! Earlier while Evan was waiting for his turn back stage, he had drunk two cases of beer and a gallon of whiskey. He had also eaten a box of Ex-lax. Evan knew the man who had put the show on. Evan's act won the show and he split the side bets with his friend."

When Iky was walking along the beach, he was very depressed. He had just gone through a nasty divorce. His ex-wife Death took Iky to the cleaners and Iky was so broke that he couldn't even pay attention. Iky saw something half buried in the sand. He reached down and pulled a goofy looking lamp out of the sand. Iky rubbed the sand off the lamp. Suddenly, a Genie came out of the lamp.

Iky asked, "What do you want? A piece of my ass too since I'm down and out?" Iky then explained his situation to the Genie. The Genie said, "I can feel your sorrow, and I will give you a very special offer. You may have three wishes, but whatever you wish for, your ex wife will get the same doubled." Iky thought about it for a while and he told the Genie, "Okay Genie, I wish I had a brand new four wheel drive truck." Suddenly poof, there is a brand-new truck in front of Iky. The Genie said, "Look into this crystal ball." Iky looked into the crystal ball and saw two trucks in front of Death's house, which Iky paid for. Iky said. "Genie, I wish I had a million dollars." Poof! There was a million dollars in front of Iky. Again, Iky looked into the crystal ball; there was two million dollars beside Death's two new trucks. Iky was not upset, as most people would be. Iky looked at the Genie with a great big grin and he said, "Genie, I wish you would take a baseball bat and beat me half to death." The Genie smiled and said, "Okay, batter up."

When Ort was in high school in Minnesota, during the summer he would work for one of the local ranchers named Jay Loren. Jay drove an old beat up pickup truck that had no side windows, and the heater did not work. In the winter months, Jay would drive his truck around and most of the time he would only wear a short-sleeved T-shirt. Jay always said the coldest he had ever been was when he was in Korea.

While Ort was out baling hay in one of the fields, he noticed that every time he passed a gate, there was something on top of the fence post. Ort wondered what it was because hundreds of flies covered it. After Ort made his next pass around, he shut the tractor off and walked over to the fence post. As Ort got up to the fence post, he saw that it was Jay's false teeth on the post. Ort got back up on the tractor and went back to work. A little while later Jay drove up to the post, brushed the flies off his false teeth, and then put them into his mouth. Jay called this the poor man's Polident.

While smoking a cigarette, Iky's friend Nathan told him, "I just got out of the hospital yesterday. Cough, cough, gag, and spit. They removed one of my lungs. Cough, cough, gag, and spit. Now I have cut my smoking in half." Iky said, "When they take your other lung out, you can quit smoking altogether."

Carol Flatchest asked Pamerrhoid Nobrains, "Do you smoke after sex?" Nobrains answered, "I don't know, I've never looked." Nobrains asked Flatchest, "Do you smoke after sex?" Flatchest answered "No, but the mailman does after he's finished." Nobrains said, "That is funny because my husband is a mailman and I have never seen him smoke after sex. Flatchest said, "That's because you have never looked."

While Iky was talking to his friend Psycho, Psycho asked, "Have I ever told you about my Uncle Jeff?" Iky asked, "Was he the one who was selling those dildos that said on the box - We might not be number one, but we are right up there?" Psycho answered, "No; that was my Uncle John. Anyway, Uncle Jeff was a traveling salesman, and while Jeff was down in Texas he had been on the road all day. Jeff pulled into this small town, drove up to the local bar, and walked in. Jeff sat down at a table. The bar maid came up to him, and he ordered a beer.

While he was waiting for his beer, Jeff looked around the place. There were a few people in there, and in the front of the bar, there was a stage with a big curtain. There was a sign above that read, "Live Entertainment." Off to the right-hand side on the stage was a man sitting with a snare drum. When the bar maid brought Jeff his beer, Jeff asked her, "What's with the live entertainment?" The bar maid answered, "Joe will be out in a little while." About five minutes passed, and then the man with the snare drum started drumming away. The curtain rose, and in the middle of the stage was a table. Lying on the table were three walnuts lined up in a row.

Joe walked out stark ass naked with a tremendous hard on. Joe stood behind the table so everybody could see. Suddenly, his hard on smashed down on the table and shattered the walnuts. Jeff finished his beer and walked out. Twenty years later Jeff stopped at the same bar. He recognized the place when he walked in because there was the same bar maid, the same man on the snare drum, and the same sign that read, "Live Entertainment." Jeff sat down at a table, the bar maid walked up to him, and he ordered a beer. Jeff asked, "When will Joe be on?" She replied, "In just a few minutes."

Suddenly the man on the snare drum started drumming away, the curtain rose, and this time there were three coconuts lined up in a row on the table. Joe was an old man now, and he was using a walker. He finally reached the table. Joe set his walker off to the side. He was holding on to the table, his hard on smashed down on the table, and shattered the coconuts. Jeff asked the bar maid, "I was here twenty years ago. Why did Joe switch from walnuts to coconuts?" The bar maid answered, "Joe has got bad eyesight." Iky said to Psycho, "When Joe goes totally blind he will probably be busting bowling balls!"

Iky asked Bigfoot, "I wonder how a blind person knows when they are finished wiping their butt?" Bigfoot answered, "You moron, that's why they have Seeing Eye Dogs." Iky said, "If they didn't have Seeing Eye Dogs, maybe they could use Bloodhounds or Brown-nosers instead."

Iky's Cousin Alex from North Dakota came down to Arkansas and spent some time with Iky. Iky's friend Roger who is an Arkie, but only on his sister's side, was there also. Alex asked, "Roger, why did Ole wear condoms on his ears?" Roger asked, "Who's Ole?" All Northerners know who Ole is. Iky said, "He is Alex's cousin." Roger asked, "Why did Ole wear condoms on his ears?" Alex answered, "So he wouldn't catch hearing aids." Roger asked Alex, "Does your cousin Ole wear hearing aids like Iky does?" Alex answered, "No, because he can't get them over his condoms."

Iky worked the graveyard shift for years, and he told everybody, "Working third shift is like Dracula and he sucks too." At that time, Iky lived in a trailer park with Bigfoot. When Iky would get off work in the mornings, he could never get any sleep. Neighbors would fire up there lawn mowers, dogs would be barking, kids yelling, cars driving by with there ghetto blasters blaring, phone ringing, water dripping in the sink, and sales men beating on his door.

He would pull all of the window shades down, just to make it dark, and nothing would work – he still couldn't sleep. It got to the point that Iky could hear a fly fart. Iky can't normally hear anything because he is deaf, but with the lack of sleep, his nerves were shot. One morning when he got off work, Iky told himself, "I am going to get some sleep today no matter what."

Iky got home and crawled into bed. He was actually getting some sleep until he heard pounding on the door. Iky lost it, jumped out of bed, and ran to the front door. He jerked the door open and yelled, "WHAT IN THE HELL DO YOU WANT!" There were two cops standing there looking at him, and the only thing Iky was wearing was his birthday suit. One cop said to the other, "Joe, call in on the radio, and tell them that we found that psycho streaker."

Iky was getting ready to go to town. He had just taken some new medications, and they had been giving him the squirts, in other words, the shits. Iky was all out of Depends so he called his neighbor Ralph, "Hey Ralph, I'm on my way to town, and I'm all out of Depends. Can I borrow one of yours?" Ralph said, "I'm sorry Iky, but I only have one left and I'm wearing it right now." Iky said, "Let me use that one, and I'll bring it back to you tonight."

Meano went to the bar with his leprechaun friend Shawn, who was only two feet tall. Several tables over was a black man named Leroy. After Meano and Shawn had drunk several pitchers, Shawn jumped off his chair, ran over to Leroy's table, pulled a chair out, and jumped on it. Then he jumped up on the table, got right in Leroy's face and he said, "Thhhhh." Slobber and spit were running down Leroy's face.

Shawn jumped down on the chair then onto the floor, and he ran back over to his table. After Shawn drank some more beer, he ran back over to Leroy's table again. He jumped up on the chair, then the table, and he is in Leroy's face again going, "Thhhhh." Shawn jumped down onto the chair, then onto the floor and back to his table he ran. He kept doing this repeatedly until Leroy finally had enough. He went over to their table, and he pulled out a great big knife. Leroy said, "The next time that little S.O.B. spits in my face, I'm going to cut his dick off!" Meano burst out laughing. Leroy asked, "What's so funny?" Meano answered, "Leprechauns don't have dicks." Leroy asked, "Then how do they piss?" Meano got in Leroy's face and said, "Thhhhh."

Big Foot said, "Jerkbob East is so fat that whenever he goes to a nude beach everybody thinks he is the Michelin Man.

Iky's friend Roger worked the graveyard shift. He had a good hiding place where he could catch some sleep. The room that Roger was using had big water and insulated steam lines running throughout the room. Roger would climb on top of one of these lines and sleep. He would always unscrew the light bulb so that if anybody turned the light switch on it wouldn't work. The room was pitch black, and the only thing you had to worry about was the supervisor Ole.

Before Ole became supervisor, Ole's nickname was Shit House Ole. He used to spend most of his time hiding in the restroom. Ole was one of the biggest loafers in the plant, so he knew where all of the hiding spots were. While Roger was sleeping, the sliding door started to open. Ole was standing there flipping the light switch on and off, but it wasn't working. Ole then pulled out his lighter and lit it up. Roger leaned over and blew it out. This went on about five times. Ole left the room and went up front. He wrote a work order to have the light fixed and the draft in that room checked out.

One day Iky was at his Mom's house. Mom asked, "Iky, I have been looking all over for my glasses. Can you help me find them?" Iky answered, "Sure Mom, you are wearing them." Mom said, "I see."

Sometimes Iky really does some dumb things like the time he was doing some carpenter work with his brother Ort, who is a building contractor. While they were working on a house Iky showed up, and Ort needed some pipe insulation. All construction workers call it by its nickname, donkey dick. Ort told Iky to go down to the hardware store and get him some donkey dick.

After six hours had gone by, Iky finally got back. Ort asked, "What took you so long?" Iky answered, "The hardware store didn't have any, and have you ever noticed that whenever you go to a store, most of the time you can never find anybody to wait on you? When I finally found somebody and I told them what you wanted I had more people help me than I have ever had before. I'll bet that I had at least twenty-five people helping me out.

They let me use their cell phones; they gave me numbers to call to see if any other stores had any. They had me calling banks, zoos, restaurants, schools, churches, abortion clinics, sperm banks, women senators, court houses, police stations, ex wife's and husbands, 911, people out of the phone book, hospitals, psychiatrists, male strip bars, and one man even had me call up that new gay bar that they just opened. I will bet I made at least five hundred and fifty phone calls. Finally, the last guy I talked to knew where I could get some."

Ort asked, "I need it right now, where is it?" Iky answered, "It's down at the sale barn, and I need to use a stock trailer to go get it." Ort yelled, "IKY, YOU DUMB S.O.B. I'M GLAD THAT I DIDN'T TELL YOU TO GET SOME ELEPHANT DICK; EVERYBODY IS GOING TO THINK THAT YOU'RE A RETARDED MORON!" Iky said, "Hey chill out, I signed your name on the ticket, I used your name on the phone, and if you are going to want me to get some elephant dick, next time you're going to need a bigger trailer."

Iky was talking to his friend Psycho a long time ago. He was telling Psycho how his wife Death was driving him crazy. Psycho had a very unique solution to Iky's problem Psycho said "Hell, O.J. her." Iky took a gallon of orange juice and dumped it over her head.

Iky walked into the new Chinese restaurant and a woman asked Iky, "Where would you like to sit?" Iky looked at her and said, "Usually I sit on my butt." Woman said, "That is not what I mean." Iky asked, "What, you do not sit on your butt?" The Chinese woman answered, "Confucius say, "Man who sits on toilet with his head is in deep shit."

Jerkbob East is so dumb that he does not use any soap or shampoo whenever he takes a shower - he uses an umbrella!

When Little Iky was in Kindergarten School, the classroom had its own bathroom. One day when Little Iky was sitting on the toilet, he started hollering his head off, "Mrs. Rudd, Mrs. Rudd!" Mrs. Rudd opened the door and asked, "What is the matter, Iky?" Little Iky asked, "Mrs. Rudd, will you wipe me?"

When Little Iky's Mom came to pick Little Iky up from school, Mrs. Rudd told her what had happened that day. Little Iky's Mom was so embarrassed she said, "How Rude." Mrs. Rudd said, "Your son is nothing but an ass wipe."

Iky was squirrel hunting, and after he got his bag limit of squirrels. Iky walked back to his house. Waiting in his yard was Meano and Dominico. Meano is from Missouri the show me state, and Dominico is from New Jersey the blow me state. These two make quite a combination when you put them together. When you put all three of these idiots together there is no telling what state of mind you will be in. Meano asked, "Hey Iky, how many squirrels did you get with that .22 rifle?" Iky answered, "I got eight this time." Dominico said, "I don't see any fuckin squirrels. What da fuck did you do? Did you fuckin eat them already?"

Iky pulled a couple of zip lock baggies out of his fanny pack. Iky had already cleaned the squirrels out in the woods. Dominico looked at them and said, "What da fuck is the matter with them fuckin squirrels? They look like they got da fuckin mange." Meano said, "Aw they are flying squirrels." Dominico said, "Flying squirrels my ass. Iky has more fuckin hair on his head than what they got on their whole fuckin bodies. Where da fuck are da feathers at?" Iky answered, "They are molting right now." Dominico asked, "What da fuck do them fuckin hairless flying squirrels do in the fuckin cold winter months?" Meano answered, "They fly down south for the winter."

One night at work Iky was getting hungry, so he went into the cafeteria. The graveyard shift could get the morning hot breakfast before they left. While Iky was standing there looking over the buffet, Deborah the cashier asked, "Hey Iky, do you want to have a good breakfast?" Iky answered, "You bet I do. Do you know where I can find one?"

A corporate Lawyer was going over some legal issues with the Human Resources Director Pamerrhoid Nobrains. After spending nearly two hours with her, the Lawyer asked Pamerrhoid, "Are you a blond?" Nobrains answered, "I don't know. I have never looked. Do you want to see?" The Lawyer used one of Clint Eastwood's famous one-liners, "Only with humans."

When Harley was in Saudi Arabia, he stopped at the local used camel dealership's lot. Ahab the Arab asked, "What kind of camel are you interested in?" Harley said, "I would like to see the best one you got." Ahab said, "Clyde is a very special camel, and I will show you what he can do." Ahab took Clyde over to the oasis that was next door. Then, Ahab pushed Clyde's head down into the water and told Harley, "Hold Clyde's head down." Ahab walked behind Clyde and grabbed Clyde's tail.

Ahab started pumping Clyde's tail up and down. Ahab said, "This is the new feature on this style. That is how you fill Clyde's hump with water." Harley said, "Here, let's trade places. I want to try that. Harley started pumping Clyde's tail like an old-fashioned water pump. After about three minutes of steady pumping Harley yelled out, "Hey Ahab you need to pick up Clyde's head about a foot, because there is either mud or oil coming out back here!"

Iky thinks that Beef Jerky is mad cow disease.

While they were having a Management Meeting at work, a big shot from Corporate was addressing the meeting. He said, "Now listen up people and pay attention." The Plant Manager Carol Flatchest asked, "About how much is this going to cost us?"

One Halloween Psycho heard a knock at the door. He opened the door and there was a little boy standing there in his costume. The little boy said, "Trick or treat." Psycho reached out and grabbed the little boy's sack of candy, went back into his trailer, and closed the door. Fifteen minutes later, there was a knock at the door. When Psycho opened the door chewing on a candy bar, an angry, ugly Mother was standing in front of him, and this was not the Father.

Psycho asked, "Where is your mask?" The mother answered, "I don't need a mask!" Psycho said, "Boy, isn't that the truth." The mother said, "My son just told me that you took his sack of candy. Is this true?" Psycho said, "Yes, that is true." The mother asked, "Why did you do that?"

Psycho answered, "Because when your son said, "Trick or treat," that's when I took his candy. That was the trick, and now I have the treat. I can give your son's empty sack back, so you can put that over your head, because you are not going to get any candy, looking the way you do." Then Psycho closed the door.

The Human Resources Director Pamerrhoid Nobrains is a unique individual; her name speaks for itself. She has no I.Q. because she has no brains. She only went to school for two and a half years, then she became a Romper Room drop out. She also thinks that a vasectomy is a large dangerous man-eating insect.

A long time ago the best Plant Manager the company ever had was Mr. Dick Monday. Mr. Monday and Pamerrhoid were having a meeting with the Maintenance Department. They were discussing an important issue about working on the air conditioners that were up on the roof.

One of the maintenance men said, "There is only one way to get up on the roof, and that is the staircase in the generator room." Nobrains asked, "If there is only one way to get up on the roof, then how do you get back down?" Mr. Monday said, "Pamerrhoid, let's move onto the next question."

Iky thinks that Tojo is that shop hand cleaner stuff used to remove grease and oil.

Iky called Bigfoot up and said, "I just bought a brand-new television set yesterday, and the darn thing doesn't work." Bigfoot asked, "Well, do you have it plugged in?" Iky answered, "Yeah, it's plugged in." Bigfoot asked, "What happens when you turn it on?" Iky answered, "The screen lights up but there's no picture, and the darn thing makes a humming sound." Bigfoot said, "Just hold on, I'm coming over to check it out."

Bigfoot drove over to Iky's place and walked into the house. Iky said, "Thanks for coming over Bigfoot. This is really aggravating because I paid a lot of money for this television set." Bigfoot asked, "Well, where is it at?" Iky answered, "It's right there on the television stand." Bigfoot said, "I know what you problem is." Iky asked, "Well, what is it?" Big Foot answered, "Your problem is that you have bought a microwave oven." Iky asked, "Well, can you fix it?" Bigfoot answered, "Yeah put a T.V. dinner in it."

Jimbob Blowme is so dumb that he thinks that Playboy is a gay magazine.

Roger's first wife Ada yelled, "You men are all nothing but a bunch of damn liars, every one of you do nothing but lie." Roger asked, "Do you know why men are liars?" She yelled, "No, why?" Roger answered, "Because men have to tell you bitches what you want to hear."

Iky was recently in Las Vegas. One night while he was playing Blackjack, a very attractive young looking woman sat down beside him. As they were playing cards and talking, they found that they had a lot in common and they were both from Minnesota.

The Babe asked Iky, "Do you have a problem with me being a Lesbian?" Iky answered, "No, I don't have a problem with that. By the way, what is a Lesbian?" The Babe answered, "Well, do you see that woman on the other side of you?"

Iky turned and looked at her, than he turned back around and he asked, "Yeah, what about her?" The Babe answered, "I would like to make love to her." Iky said, "I would like to make love to her too. So that must make me a Lesbian too."

Iky's Dad grew up during the Depression; that was when everybody was very depressed. Dad was just a little boy at the time. He would have to walk the railroad tracks to and from Rogers, North Dakota, and he had to walk through the Hobo camps that were along the railroad tracks.

Now for you younger people that don't know what a Hobo is, a Hobo is a home less man. That reminds me of that old joke. What's the difference between a Hobo and a Homo? Well, a Hobo doesn't have any friends, and a Homo has friends coming out of his ass. Now, where were we? Oh yeah, Dad said the hobos terrified him. I think the homos terrify me. I guess Dad and I had something in common.

Most of the time the Hobos would go to peoples houses and beg for food, or they might steal stuff out of the gardens. Wherever a hobo camp was, there would always be a stew pot cooking. Dad said every time he went through one of them camps, if nobody was around he would add some North Dakota seasoning into their stew pots. Dad would take a leak in them.

Iky was at the Kentucky Fried Chicken restaurant. While he was sitting at the table eating the new Buffalo wings, the manager walked over to Iky and asked, "How do you like these Buffalo wings?" Iky said, "Well actually, I thought this buffalo meat would taste a little different. It kind of reminds me of chicken."

Iky said, "Jerkbob East is so fat that every time he goes to the beach the sun bathers put on winter coats."

When Iky was taking a break at work, he was sitting in the cafeteria. Well, Hue Burt walked in and sat down at the same table. I will tell you about Hue Burt. He is the friendliest person that you will ever meet, and he will do anything for you. Hue Burt looks like a brick outhouse; in other words, he does not have to take any shit from anybody.

While they were eating Hue Burt asked, "Iky you have fought in Tough Man Fights, and you have won them. I have fought in them five times now and I have not won any yet. Will you please tell me your secret?" Iky answered, "Well Hue Burt, there is no secret. You are supposed to knock out your opponent, not the referee." So Hue Burt thought about it and said, "Next time I'll knock out the judges too."

Iky's distant relative Barry is originally from North Dakota too, but he lives in Kansas now. Whenever Iky goes to Barry's house, all he has to do is follow the beer cans. One day Barry came down and spent some time with Iky. They got hungry so they went to the Mexican restaurant.

As they sat down the waiter asked, "What do you want to drink?" Barry asked, "What?" Iky answered, "He wants to know what you want to drink." After a while, the waiter came back and asked, "What would you like to order?" Barry asked, "What?" Iky answered, "He wants to know what you want to order." A little while later, the waiter came back and asked them, "Would you like anything else?" Barry asked, "What?" Iky answered, "He wants to know if you want anything else." After about five minutes had gone by Barry said, "I didn't know that you could speak Spanish, Iky." Iky answered, "I don't." Barry asked, "Then how did you know what the waiter was talking about?" Iky answered, "Because I know how to read lips."

As Iky was traveling on his way to see his cousin Alex in North Dakota, he had been on the road for twelve hours. Iky realized that he had forgotten to bring his medication along, and it was at home in Arkansas. He began to feel a major, not a sergeant, manic episode coming on, and he started to panic. Iky grabbed his cell phone and called his psychiatrist. Everything worked out just fine, because Iky did what his psychiatrist told him to do. He drove to the nearest McDonalds and ordered a Happy Meal.

Pamerrhoid Nobrains thinks a Condom is a dumb convict. Flatchest thinks it is a building where rich people live.

Carol Flatchest thinks a Rectum is a person who has been in a car wreck. Nobrains thinks it is a person who has just had brain surgery.

Iky told Psycho, "Money can't buy you everything." Psycho said, "Yeah, but it sure pays the bills."

When Iky was married to Death, he cut an article out of the paper. Iky took it home and showed it to Death. It was a quotation by the famous comedian Pat Paulson that read, "The best way to save you from going through the heartache and pain of a divorce is to find a woman you hate and buy her a house." Death looked at him and said, "You never bought me a house."

When Iky was at a party one night, a woman pulled out a big bag of pot. Iky asked, "Where did you get that?" She answered, "I got it from Juan Valdez." Iky asked, "You're going to smoke some coffee?" The woman said, "It's not coffee, it's pot." Iky said, "Now I understand. Old Juan wasn't making enough money selling coffee, so he switched over to growing and selling pot, huh?"

When Iky got his electric bill in the mail, it was $752.00. He almost freaked out. Iky got on the phone and called the electric company. He talked to a secretary and she assured Iky the bill was a mistake. She told him she would get everything straightened out. Iky said, "Thank you, I almost had a heart attack when I saw that bill. It was almost like putting your finger in a light socket, and it was very electrifying." The secretary said, "Yes, I know that electric bill was very shocking."

Willa Mae says, "An excuse is just a propped up lie."

Five Beers was over at Meano's house one night. The reason his name is Five Beers is because he cannot handle six beers. While they were sitting there getting gooned up, Meano's German Shepard dog, Nola walked into the living room and lay down. Nola began to lick and clean her private parts. Chief looked at the dog and said, "Boy, I sure wish that I could do that." Meano said, "Well, I can hold the dog for you."

At work, they did not allow chewing tobacco in the plant, but several people were doing it anyway, and some of them were spitting everywhere. One of the workers named Bill was a dipper, and his locker was right next to Iky's locker. Every night when Iky was changing into his work clothes, Bill would show up like clockwork the same time every night. Iky was telling Harvey about how he did not like the dippers spitting all over the plant. Harvey gave Iky some advice on what to do about the situation.

The next night when Iky was changing into his work clothes, Bill showed up right on time. He grabbed his combination lock in his left hand, and worked the combination with his right hand. The lock opened and he took it off the handle and set it on the bench. Bill opened the door and reached inside to grab a can of Copenhagen. He took the lid off, set it down, and then got a big pinch of chew. Bill put the Copenhagen in his mouth.

Right then he got a whiff of Jiff, his nose curled up, and he had a strange look on his face. Bill put the can up to his nose and smelled it. Then he checked out the expiration date on the can. He put the can back into his locker and went back to work. Iky had taken a nasty smelling hunter cover scent and sprayed it all over Bill's combination lock. They called the scent fox piss.

When Bigfoot was into motocross cycle racing, Iky and Marty Mouth were at the track watching the races. Bigfoot's heat race started and there were about ten competitors. As the motorcycles were screaming by, about four laps later, the leader was ahead of everyone. Iky said, "Man, that guy is in a class by himself." A little while later Bigfoot went by, and he was in last place. Marty said, "Yeah and Bigfoot is in a class by himself too!"

Carol Flatchest walked into Pamerrhoid Nobrains office and saw Nobrains jumping rope. Flatchest asked, "How long have you been jumping rope Pamerrhoid?" Nobrains answered, "I have been doing this for six hours straight and I have two more hours to go." Flatchest asked, "Is this a part of your new exercise program?" Nobrains answered, "No, Corporate told me to skip a day." Flatchest said, "Corporate sent me an e-mail a week ago and I still have not received it. I think they forgot to put a stamp on the letter."

Iky had an appointment with Doctor Cross and his Mom went with him. Iky had one of those electronic fart machines in the pocket of his windbreaker. (Hey, talk about blowing wind!) When the Doctor came into the room, he asked Iky, "How are you doing, Iky?" Iky answered, "Well Doc, this medication that you have prescribed me is giving me really bad gas." Right then Iky pushes the fart control button and a small fart fills the room. Iky says, "The Moexipril gives me an upset stomach." More fart sounds appear to come from Iky. He says, "The Simvastatin gives me diarrhea so bad that I have wiped my butt so much that it is bleeding." This time there are several farts followed by sounds like shitting your pants.

The Doc asked, "Iky, have you tried any of that Beano anti gas medicine?" Iky was pushing the fart control button constantly while he answered, "No, I haven't tried that stuff." Iky's Mom began laughing and she finally couldn't take it anymore. She told the doctor, "He's got a fart machine." Iky took it out of his pocket and showed it to his doctor. His doctor said, "It wasn't that I didn't think that was funny. I'm just not feeling so well right now." Iky asked, "I'm sorry to hear that. Do you think that you need to see a doctor?" Suddenly loud farts fill the room again. Iky's Mom said, "Iky! I told you to put that thing away!" Iky said, "That was not the fart machine."

Tommy asked Iky, "Did you hear about the Fortune Teller's husband?" Iky asked, "No, what about him?" Tommy answered, "He's got crystal balls." Iky asked Tommy, "Did you hear about the Pro Bowler's wife?" Tommy asked, "No, what about her?" Iky answered,

"She had three strikes against him, and he couldn't even pick up a spare so she found herself a better pair of balls."

Iky's friend Greg was at a bar one day drinking a few beers and minding his own business. A woman sat down beside him and said, "If I were only twenty years younger." Greg looked at her and said, "Yeah, even so you would still be fat and ugly."

Iky was in the break room reading a book when Jim Bob Blowme and Jerkbob East walked in. Jerkbob said, "Hey Iky, put your hard hat back on, I'm getting blinded by the light." Blowme said, "Yeah Iky, you look like a bone head." These two morons were laughing and Iky said, "If you don't like it, then start wearing sun glasses." They sat down at a table nearby Iky. While Iky was reading, he was listening to their conversation. Jerkbob said, "I have tried five different diet programs now and the only thing that's happening is I am gaining more weight."

Iky's break was over so he got up and walked over to their table and said, "Hey Jerkoff." Jerkbob said, "That's Jerkbob." Iky said, "That's what I said. I know how you can lose twenty ugly pounds of worthless fat." Jerkbob got excited and asked, "How?" Iky answers, "You go down to the hospital and have them cut your head off. They can also remove your butt cheeks and stick them where your head was. That way your breath will still smell the same and then you can make a real ass of yourself. As Iky was walking out of the break room Blowme asked Jerkbob, "I wonder if that would really work."

Many years ago at work, Willy McFathead was working in the kitchen. It was in the middle of the summer, and it was extremely hot in the plant. That day Willy had to mix up pineapple juice. Usually the pineapple juice came in forty-pound boxes. The company started buying it in bulk, so now it came in wooden plastic lined crates, which weighed two thousand pounds. Willy had to have a small stepladder to reach the top of the box so he could take it off. He cut the plastic in the crate and draped it over the sides of the box.

Willy would climb up the stepladder, take a five-gallon bucket, and fill it with pineapple juice. While Willy was lifting the bucket out of the wooden crate, his apron was getting pineapple juice all over it. Willy's face was beet red because he was so hot, sweaty, and angry. Roy was working up on the tanks and was watching Willy. He felt sorry for him, so Roy went and got a big portable fan for Willy. Roy set the fan up behind Willy, plugged it in and turned it on. At that moment, the hurricane winds from this giant fan blew Willy's apron straight up and back over the top of Willy's head. The sticky pineapple juice apron was stuck to his face and to the top and back of his head. Willy was cussing up a storm but you could not understand a word he said because his face looked like it was stuck on flypaper!

One day Iky was walking along the beach and he found a strange looking lamp. Iky didn't know what it was so he took a leak in it. Then an angry wet Genie appeared before him. Iky asked, "Who are you? What do you want?" The Genie answered, "I am the Genie of the lamp, and you have just pissed me off." Iky said, "Well it's better to be pissed off than pissed on." The Genie said, "I know, I do not like your attitude and what you have just done to me. Ordinarily, I would grant you three wishes, but you are going to get just one wish." Iky said, "I do not like your attitude and what you have just done to me. Genie, I wish that you will go back into your lamp for all eternity." The Genie disappeared back into his lamp. Iky shouted into the spout, "Your Christmas gift is on its way!" Iky then took a big dump in the lamp and buried it in the sand.

Last New Years Eve, Iky, Bigfoot, and Toots were at Mom's place. Toots and Mom were trying to talk Bigfoot into going with them to the Eagles Club that night. Iky wouldn't go because of two reasons; the first reason is those clubs are just too noisy for him. Whenever someone tried to talk to him, Iky couldn't hear what they were saying, and this was very aggravating for him. The second reason that Iky doesn't like to go is that he doesn't want to be responsible for all of the divorces in the world. After talking to Bigfoot for about twenty minutes, Toots said, "Hey Bigfoot, we can even have Mom be the designated driver." Iky said, "Now he definitely won't go."

Iky was sitting in his living room and the phone rang. He answered the phone and a man said, "My name is Jim Abrams. I represent The National Blind Association. We are a nonprofit organization; we rely strictly on individual donations. Would you be interested in making a donation today?" Iky said, "I would really like to help you out, but I am on a fixed income, and I cannot give very much." Jim said, "I see, we would appreciate any amount." Iky said, "I thought you were blind." Iky hung the phone up.

Iky says, "When it comes to eating food, it is better to leave it than to heave it." Iky also says, "Birth control is when you go out with ugly women."

One night at work, a bunch of people were sitting in the locker room. Little Man started telling a story about when he was in the military. He began, "Back in 1969, I volunteered for the U.S. Marine Corps. I was eighteen and I had just gotten out of high school. Three days into Basic Training, we were waiting for the nightly inspection. Everybody was standing on top of their footlockers. We were only wearing underwear and everyone had there arms extended in front of them. The Drill Instructor started at one end of the barracks and worked his way to the other end. When it was your turn, the Drill Instructor would look you over. He would nod his head then you would flip your hands over. We didn't dare look around because there were two other Drill Instructors watching everybody."

Little Man continued the story, "As I was waiting for my turn, I could see the Drill Instructor out of the corner of my eye. He was about four guys from my left. Suddenly, he stopped walking. I could see him bending down and looking at something. He straightened back up and then he sidestepped and bent down again. All the while, he was looking at something. I was wondering what in the world he was doing. The Drill Instructor yelled out, "Private Switzer, do my eyes deceive me or do you have a hard on? Now, which one of you ladies is the sheep?" Switzer was standing there with a tremendous boner. The Drill Instructor shouted, "I want everybody out of the barracks right now!" The other Drill Instructors roared, "Move it, move it, get out of the barracks!" All of us rushed outside and they closed the door. I was thinking to myself that they must have been beating the living tar out of Switzer. We should have been in our bunks because it was after eight."

"I heard the Drill Instructor in the barracks shout, "Send one in!" They opened the door and each of us privates ran into the barracks one at a time. The Drill Instructor shouted out to us, "Get over here now!" We would each run over to him and stand at attention. Private Switzer was still standing on his footlocker. The Drill Instructor shouted at us "Drop your drawers and bend over!" As we bent over, Private Switzer was looking at our bare butts. The Drill Instructor shouted, "Private Switzer, does that look good to you?" Switzer yelled, "Sir, no Sir." The Drill Instructor shouted, "Next!" Another Private rushed in and the Drill Instructor asked the same question repeatedly. The Drill Instructor shouted, "Does that look good to you, Private Switzer?" Switzer answered, "Sir, no Sir." The Drill Instructor finally shouted, "Well, it's starting to look good to me!"

Iky recently walked into the police station and told the Officer behind the desk, "I would like to file murder charges." The Officer asked with great concern, "Murder? Against whom? How exactly did this person commit murder?" Iky said, "I want to file charges against the drug companies." The Officer asked, "Why do you want to file murder charges against the drug companies?" Iky answered, "The price that I have to pay for my medications is killing me."

Alex was walking along a beach and he found a magic lamp. He began to rub it. A Genie appeared before him and said, "I will grant you a wish." Alex said, "I thought a Genie was supposed to grant you three wishes." The Genie said, "That's just in the movies." Alex said, "Well Genie, with the price of everything nowadays, I can't even afford Viagra anymore. So, I wish that my penis would drag the ground." The

Genie said, "Your wish has been granted." Alex looked down and his legs were two inches long!

Iky said, "Will Rogers never met Jimbob Blowme or Jerkbob East."

A long time ago Iky's friend Psycho was driving to Little Rock on weekends to spend time with his new girlfriend. One evening he took her to a very fancy restaurant. After they had finished the meal, Psycho left five dollars on the table. Psychos' girlfriend said, "That sure is a lot of money to be leaving for a tip. Psycho said, "No, that is customary. You leave a tip that is fifteen percent of the bill."

His girlfriend said, "That is still too much money to be leaving for a tip." Psycho said, "No, that is the right amount for the tip." His girlfriend said, "You want to make love to that waitress." Psycho said, "No, I just left her a tip." His girlfriend continued complaining, "Well, I know that you want to make love to her, and I don't like the way you've been looking at my daughter, sister and mother lately either. I know that you want to make love to them too!"

Psycho said, "Well actually, I prefer young boys instead." That took care of that relationship. After Psycho told Iky this story, Iky said, "You should have had rodeo sex with her." Psycho asked, "What's that?" Iky answered, "That is when you are in the middle of making love, and you tell her that she screws just as good as her sister. Now you see if you can hang on for ten seconds." Psycho said, "Her mother bucked me off in five seconds."

Management is like a room full of drunks. They do not know how they got there, what they said, or even where they are going.

Iky's friend Skip had bought a horse from one of the local ranchers. After he got the horse home, Skip noticed the horse was blind. Skip was very angry. He told his Dad he was going to take the horse back to the rancher and get his money back. Skip's Dad said, "If you are dumb enough to buy a blind horse, that's just too bad because it's yours now." When Iky heard what happened, he told Skip, "Look at the bright side. You won't have to buy any blinders for that horse."

Mom and Dad were discussing their new cell phones. Mom told Dad she didn't understand some of the new features on the phone. Dad asked her "How would I know anything about this thing?" Then Iky walked into the room. He heard what Dad just said and he told his mom, "Here Mom, give me the phone. I know how it works." Mom handed Iky the cell phone, and he opened it up. He said, "You open the cell phone up like this, then you talk into this end of the phone and you listen on the other end."

Dad said, "Iky, you are an Einstein." Iky said, "Well thank you Dad, but what's that?" Dad said, "He was the smartest man in the world." Iky thought for a while and said, "Oh yeah, you mean Albert don't you?" Dad said, "That's amazing! You know who he was." Iky said, "Well, everybody knows Prince Albert." Dad asked, "What are you talking about?" Iky answered, "That's the guy you're talking about when you call up a grocery store, and ask if they have Prince Albert in a can. Then they usually say that they do. Then you tell them they better let him out because he needs some air." Mom said, "I worked twenty two years in a grocery store and I never saw a guy in a can." Dad said, "That's because they were in the men's room."

Iky's friend Lips who lives in Minnesota had stopped in a bar in a Finnish town. He was minding his own business and drinking a beer. A local Finlander started giving Lips a hard time. Lips asked him, "What is the closest thing to a fish's ass?" The Finlander asked, "I don't know, what?" Lips answered, "A Fin."

Carol Flatchest and Pamerrhoid Nobrains are so dumb that they report embezzled money to the I.R.S. while they wait in jail for their tax refunds.

Back in the old western days, Iky's great-great-great-Grandpa was in a saloon drinking whiskey. He was looking out the window and he could see a cowboy riding up on a horse. When the cowboy got to the saloon, he got off his horse. He walked behind the horse, raised the horse's tail up with one hand, took his other hand and stuck his finger up the horse's butt. When the cowboy pulled his finger out there was a bunch of horse crap on his finger and he rubbed it all over his lips.

He walked into the saloon, bought a drink and sat down at a table. Grandpa walked over to the cowboy and said, "Mister, you mind if I sit with you?" The cowboy said, "Go ahead, I could use some company." After they had a few drinks, Grandpa said, "Mister, I know it's none of my business, but why did you smear that horse crap all over your lips?" The cowboy said, "Chapped lips." Grandpa asked, "Chapped lips?" The cowboy said, "Yeah, it sure keeps you from licking them."

Alex told Iky the story about the horny hawk. There was a hawk flying around one day. The hawk was extremely horny. As the hawk was flying, he looked down and saw a meadowlark sitting on a fence post. The horny hawk swooped down, grabbed the meadowlark, and took it behind a bush. Well, the bush started shaking; leaves and feathers were flying everywhere. The hawk flew off, the meadowlark staggered out from behind the bush, and she said, "I'm a lark, I've been sparked, and I liked it."

The horny hawk didn't get enough and he was still horny. While he was flying around, he saw a morning dove on a tree limb. He swooped down, grabbed the dove, and took it behind a bush. The bush was shaking, leaves and feathers were flying everywhere. The hawk flew off, and the dove staggered out from behind the bush and she said, "I'm a dove, I've been loved, and I liked it."

The horny hawk was still horny, so he continued to look down while he was flying around. He saw a duck swimming in a pond down below. The hawk swooped down, grabbed the duck, and took it behind a bush. Well, the bush was shaking, leaves and feathers were flying everywhere. The hawk flew off, and the duck staggered out from behind the bush and he said, "I'm a drake, there's been a mistake and I did not like it!"

Iky said, "Many years ago Management personnel used to answer questions. These days, Management personnel always ask questions." That is their way of taking your ideas and using them as their own.

Iky's first wife Death always kept on hounding Iky about getting a boob job. Iky would always tell her no for two reasons. The first reason was he knew he would have to pay for it, and the second reason was a boob job wouldn't do Iky any good when he always had to wear a blindfold anyway. One day Death said, "If I had a boob job you wouldn't be looking at other women." Iky said, "Ever since I married you, I've been looking at other men without the blindfold."

Ort's stepson Billyjoe Jeffbob is a Rebel on his mom's side and he is a Damn Yankee on Ort's side, which is the right side of Ort's boot. Jeffbob is building a house over in Oklahoma. That reminds me of that old joke. What do a tornado and a divorce have in common in Oklahoma? Somebody is going to lose a trailer house. Oh, I forgot that is supposed to be in Arkansas. In Oklahoma, it is a chicken coop.

On weekends Ort, Bigfoot, and Iky would go over and help Jeffbob work on his house. On the way to Jeffbob's house right as you cross into Oklahoma, you pass one of Jeffbob's highly intelligent Okie neighbors, Hillbilly Bob. Nobody can figure out what language he speaks because nobody can understand what he's saying.

Hillbilly Bob's wife has a tough job. She goes and gets their food stamps once a month out of the mailbox. Have you ever seen that movie Star Wars? They had a character called Jaba the Hut. Hillbilly Bobs wife's name is Jobless the Hut. One evening while Jeffbob was driving by Hillbilly Bob's house, he saw Hillbilly Bob working on his A. T. V. so he decided to stop in. Jeffbob asked, "What are you doing Hillbilly?" Hillbilly Bob answered, "I'm trying to milk this cow and there isn't any milk coming out." Jeffbob said, "That's because it's a male."

Iky's wife Maryjane Hemply had moved to Fort Smith, Arkansas many years before they met. She had two house cats named Poncho and Tigger. Her parents came down one weekend and spent a couple of nights with her. Before they all went to bed, Maryjane's mother Wanda, took her false teeth out, placed them in a glass and had them soaking in bleach water on the bathroom cabinet.

The next morning when they got up, Wanda couldn't find her teeth where she put them the night before. They looked everywhere and wondered what had happened to them. After several hours had gone by Maryjane was still looking around the house. She just happened to glance down. Maryjane said, "Momma, I found your teeth." Wanda asked, "Well, where are they at?" Maryjane said, "They are right here under my roll-top desk. Wanda walked over to where Maryjane was standing and there sticking half buried out of the cat litter box were her false teeth. Maryjane's Dad Bill said, "Well, look at the bright side." Wanda asked, "How could there possibly be a bright side to this?" Bill answered, "If the car keys come up missing at least we know where to look." As Wanda was cleaning off her teeth, she said, "No shit."

Alex's brother Eddie who lives in California had heard the story about how Iky had forgot his medication on a road trip. Iky was freaking out until his psychiatrist told him to go to McDonald's and order a happy meal. Well, Eddie was out of Viagra, so he thought that he would try the same thing that Iky did. Eddie went to Burger King and he ordered a Whopper, and it worked!

Iky said, "Did you hear the one about the buck who went to the bank? The buck told the teller, "I'm looking for a little doe."

Iky needed to talk to his supervisor Ironbox about issues that needed to be resolved. He walked into the supervisor's office and she wasn't in there. As Iky was leaving, he saw his friend Phil in his office so Iky walked over and knocked on his door. Phil said, "Come on in." Iky walked in and sat down. Iky said, "Phil, I have a problem." Phil said, "Tell me about it and I'll see if I can help you." Iky said, "I've been married for two years now and it's been a good two years. Lately I have not been able to satisfy my wife, and I would not blame her if she left me. It's as if I'm playing in a baseball game. It's my turn to bat, I'm standing on the plate, and I look down and see that I don't have my bat with me. That is down right embarrassing." Phil said, "Iky, that happens to everyone at one time or another. There's no reason to be ashamed of it."

Phil was very concerned and sympathetic. Iky said, "I thought it was only happening to me. I'm glad I can to talk to you about it." Phil said, "If you have any problems Iky, just come on in and we can talk about it." Iky said, "Okay Phil, this is what I had in mind. I've talked it over with my wife and my doctor too. I feel this will help me out, not only mentally, but sexually as well." Phil asked, "Well, what are you going to do?" Iky answered, "I'm going to have a sex change operation, so that Ironbox and I can become lovers." The concerned look on Phil's face started to melted away, he raised one hand and said, "Wait a minute, just wait a minute." He reached down, picked up his trashcan and he dumped the contents on the floor. Then he put the trashcan over his head and burst out laughing.

Iky was at the bank when Debbie the teller asked him, "Iky, would you be interested in a CD?" Iky thought she had asked if he were interested in VD. Iky said, "Well, thank you Debbie for the offer. I know that you're a nice girl. I don't mean to hurt your feelings, but I don't think I want any of that stuff." Debbie said, "Iky, the thing about a CD is that after several years they grow."

Iky said, "That's what I'm afraid of. How big can it get?" Debbie said, "That all depends on how much interest you put into it." Iky said, "I don't think I'm in that good of shape." Debbie said, "Don't worry

Iky. We can fluctuate your interest." Iky asked, "When you say we, how many people are you talking about?" Debbie answered, "As many as it takes." Iky said, "That sounds like it could hurt." Debbie said, "Yes it could hurt if you pull it out too soon because you could lose the interest or the principal."

Iky said, "As far as losing interest, I'm not very worried about that. A magazine or a movie can bring that back. As far as the principal goes, we don't need him because I haven't seen him in a long time. I don't think I need a thumping or to stand in a corner. Debbie, this is what I will do. I'll get a second opinion then I'll get back with you on this issue. I'm not interested in any VD until I talk to Dr. Ruth first." Iky turned around and walked out of the bank.

Iky walked into a large hardware store. He had to go to the bathroom very badly. He asked an employee named Dave, "Where are the restrooms?" Dave told Iky, "The restrooms are at the end of aisle eleven." Iky thought he said aisle seven so he walked down aisle seven. Dave started to notice a large group of people gathering around aisle seven.

Dave went over and he saw Iky sitting on a demo toilet, Dave ran over to Iky and yelled, "I told you aisle eleven, not aisle seven!" Iky said, "Hey chill out, you have two problems here." Dave screamed, "What in the world are you talking about?" Iky said, "First, I don't have any toilet paper and second, all these other eight toilets are backed up too."

If you are a full time worker and get hurt, they send you to a hospital. If you are a temporary worker and get hurt, they send you out the back door.

One day Bigfoot asked Iky, "Why wasn't Jesus born in Mexico?" Iky answered, "I don't know, was it because he couldn't speak Spanish?" Bigfoot said, "No, because they couldn't find three wise men and a virgin." Iky said, "Well Jesus wouldn't have been born in Arkansas then." Bigfoot asked, "Why not?" Iky answered, "Because Bill Clinton took care of all the virgins in Arkansas."

When Iky's Dad died, he went with his Mom, Toots, and Bigfoot to the funeral home to arrange to have his Dad cremated. The one thing about funeral homes - people are just dying to get in there. While the family was discussing the arrangements, the funeral director was so sympathetic; it was as if he could fill their loss as well.

Iky said, "Dad always said when he kicked the bucket the undertaker could have his gold tooth." Mom said to the undertaker, "That's right, you can have Dad's gold tooth." The undertaker said, "No, we don't do that because the law requires that you will get all of your loved ones remains. Excuse me; I have to go get some papers that need to be signed."

The undertaker left the room, and everyone sat there in dead silence. Iky said, "Do you know what he is doing right now?" Bigfoot asked, "What?" Iky answered, "He is looking in his stash of teeth trying to find Dad's gold tooth, and put it back in his mouth."

One night after work, Iky stopped over at Bigfoot's house. Bigfoot noticed that Iky had a big brown spot on the back of his pants. Bigfoot started laughing at Iky. Iky said, "You can laugh all you want to, but this is free advertising." Bigfoot asked, "How does walking around with a big brown spot on the back of your pants have anything to do with advertising?" Iky said, "It's like that UPS commercial that says, 'What can Brown do for you?'"

Iky's uncle Dennis lives in Arizona. He keeps in touch with Iky all the time because he is the only one who understands Iky's illness. In other words, he is a normal dumb ass just like Iky. While they were having a conversation on the phone Dennis said, "I'm suffering from Alzheimer's." Iky said, "I'm really sorry to hear that, do I know you?

Whom am I speaking to?" Dennis said, "This is your dumb ass uncle." Iky asked, "Which one?" Dennis answered, "The dumb one." Iky asked, "Oh, this must be dumb ass Dennis. What's Alzheimer's?"

Dennis answered, "It's a disease. You suffer with memory loss and the older you get, the worse it gets." Iky said, "I'm really sorry to hear that you have Alzheimer's, but look at the bright side." Dennis asked, "What is the bright side?" Iky answered, "Someday, when you don't know who you are, you'll be able to stand in front of a mirror and have an intelligent conversation with a total stranger." Dennis said, "Hey I like that by the way, who am I talking to?" Iky answered, "This is your dumb ass nephew." Dennis asked, "Which one?" Iky answered, 'The dumb one." Dennis said, "Oh, I must be talking to Toots."

Iky's new neighbor Paul is from North Dakota also. Paul is building his house and shop himself and Iky has been helping him. Paul's wife is still up in Fargo working at a fence company. One morning Iky walked up to Paul's house and the front door was wide open. Iky walked into the house. Paul was standing on a chair, there was rope hanging from the ceiling, and the other end of the rope tied around Paul's stomach.

Iky asked, "What in the world are you doing, Paul?" Paul answered, "I'm getting very lonely being out here in the boonies by myself, and I miss my wife." Iky said, "Paul, if you're going to hang yourself, you're supposed to put the rope around your neck, not your stomach." Paul said, "I tried that, but then I couldn't breathe."

Iky's friend Boris is quite a character from Alabama. Boris said, "The worst beating that I ever had was when I was five years old. I was staying with my Grandma. That night when we went to bed I was sleeping with her. I got horny and tried to hump her. She beat the living tar out of me." Iky said, "I guess you were just trying to keep it in the family, Boris."

Iky said to be a sewer man reminded him of that old movie 'My Name Is Nobody.' In the movie, Henry Fonda said, "When you are up to your neck in shit, you keep your mouth shut."

Management thinks Gatorade is a charity organization that takes up donations for homeless alligators down in the Bayou.

One winter Iky was having problems with his new wood stove. He called Ort and asked him if he would come out and look at it. Ort told him he would be on his way." When Ort drove into Iky's yard, all of the doors and the windows were wide open and there was smoke pouring out of them. Ort noticed that there was no smoke coming out of the chimney. As he ran into the house Iky said, "Boy, I'm sure glad to see you because I don't know what to do."

Ort checked the wood stove carefully and he said, "Iky, I have some good news and some bad news for you." Iky said, "Tell me the good news first." Ort said, "The good news is that your wood stove is all right, the bad news is that I'm going to have to put in a new stove pipe." Iky said, "That's not so bad." Ort said, "Yeah, but I have to hook it up to your electric stove."

Iky went to see his psychiatrist, and his psychiatrist asked Iky to tell him a story. Iky began to tell him a very long-winded story. After an hour had gone by, the alarm on the psychiatrist watch went off, and he said, "Okay, your times up." Iky asked him, "Don't you want to hear the rest of my story?" The psychiatrist replied, "That won't be necessary."

Iky looked at him and asked, "Why not Doc?" The psychiatrist answered, "I have heard you tell that same story fifteen times." Angrily Iky asked, "Why didn't you tell me when I started my story?" The psychiatrist got up off the couch, took his sunglasses off, and looking at Iky, he said, "Because I needed the nap and the hundred dollars."

When Jerkbob East was born, he was so ugly that the Doctor slapped himself, and then he began to protest for abortions. Jerkbob was so ugly that he became the poster boy for birth control, and to this day, he still is.

Iky had some new prescriptions from his regular doctor and his psychiatrist. He went to the local drug store to get them filled. Don, the Pharmacist said, "These medications have many side effects like dizziness, memory loss, weight gain, and sleeping disorders." Iky said, "Those are some bad side effects." Don said, "Those are the good side effects." Iky asked, "Then what are the bad side effects?" Don said, "The price that you are going to have pay for this stuff."

Meano told Iky, "I have a poem that I like and I will tell you."

"A man works."
"A man sweats."
"A man dies."
"Almost as fast."
"As the sweat dries."

Iky told Meano, "That guy needs to use some deodorant. That reminds me of what General Douglas Macarthur said. He said that 'Old soldiers never die they just smell that way.'" Meano said, "Iky he said, 'Old soldiers never die they just fade away.'" Iky said, "That might be what he said, but I know some old soldiers who sure smell like they have died and that smell doesn't fade away."

When Iky was in grade school, he occasionally done mean things. There was the time he took a chunk of old fashion chocolate flavored Ex-Lax from the medicine cabinet at home to school. When the bus dropped Iky off at school that morning, Iky ran across the street to Thomas's Grocery Store and he bought some red licorice. The licorice was hollow and Iky bit the end off one of them. Then Iky took the Ex-Lax and shoved it inside the licorice. Iky went back to school. As Iky was walking down the hall, he was chewing on some licorice. Back in those days, a very popular toy was the Mr. Potato Head Doll; there were different attachments that came with the doll, so you could change it into different characters.

One of the kids at school looked just like the Mr. Potato head toy because his head was oblong shaped, so his nickname was Potatohead. Well, Potatohead saw that Iky was chewing on some licorice, and he asked Iky if he could have some. Iky handed him the loaded licorice. Potatohead saw the Ex-Lax in the end of the licorice so he was going to break it off and throw it away. Iky said, "Wait a minute, this is a new kind of licorice that is chocolate filled." Therefore, Potatohead went ahead and ate it. The school bell rang and everybody went to his or her classes.

When the school bell rang for the start of the second class, the halls were full of kids. Iky had to take a leak so he walked into the nearest restroom. As Iky was opening the door and starting to walk in, he suddenly froze in terror. Standing in front of Iky was Potatohead. His pants were pulled down to his ankles and he had shit running out of his butt. Mrs. Rudd was trying to clean him up as best as she could. There was at least one whole roll of shit covered paper towels lying on the floor. Iky turned around and Beef was standing behind him. Beef asked, "What's the matter, Iky?" Iky said, "We can't go in there right now because Potatohead has got mashed potatoes and brown gravy running out of his butt." Beef said, "No shit. Maybe if we wait long enough, Potatohead might start serving some lettuce too."

While Elian was working, she climbed up a portable staircase on wheels. As she got ready to dump a box of glue chips into the machine, John ran over and pulled her pants down. Elian was standing there in her panties. She pulled her pants up and ran out the door. She went to the front of the plant and barged into the Plant Manager's office.

Elian yelled, "I want John fired after what he has just done to me! It was so embarrassing! I have never been so humiliated in my life!" Mr. Monday was thinking that John has done something terrible to her, so he asked, "Elian, what did John do to you?" Elian screamed, "He pulled my pants down and then he wouldn't fuck me!" Mr. Monday is still laughing his ass off.

One day after Iky got married to Death, he began to get very suspicious of her. When they were making love, she would scream out her Dad's name and then she would say, "Oh, he's just a friend." At that time, Death's daughter was also living with her and Iky. One afternoon Iky heard knocking at the front door. He went to the door, and there was a man standing there with a bouquet of flowers. Iky said, "I'll get Death's daughter for you." The man said, "That won't be necessary because I'm here for Death." Iky handed the man a hundred dollars, a pack of cigarettes, and the blind fold. Iky said, "Don't bring her back." Two days later, the man brought Death back. He gave Iky two hundred dollars, a carton of cigarettes, and two blindfolds. He told Iky, "I can't take anymore of this. When we would make love she would yell out her sister's name." Iky asked, "Which one?" The man answered, "All of them!"

At work one night, Iky asked Tommy, "Were you ever in the service?" Tommy answered, "Yes, I was in the Army from 1967 until 1970." Iky asked, "Were you ever in combat?" Tommy answered, "Our unit was in twenty-two major engagements and countless skirmishes. Some of our battles were even hand-to-hand confrontations with fixed bayonets; we were overrun seven times and had to call in air strikes several times. Those battles were very bloody and ugly. Our unit suffered seventy percent casualties; we had orders not to take any prisoners." Iky asked, "Were you ever wounded?" Tommy answered, "I received two purple hearts and a bronze star." Iky asked, "Golly Tommy, Vietnam was really tough, huh?" Tommy answered, 'No, our unit didn't go to Nam. We were controlling the race rioters and the peace protesters here in the states."

The last year Iky was in Minnesota, he got into a new advanced boxing training program. Back then, the big pro fighter was Roberto Duran. His nickname was 'Hands of Stone.' Duran could punch his way through brick buildings without having his hands wrapped and without wearing bag gloves. At that time, Iky had built up quite a reputation for being able to absorb tremendous amounts of punishment in the ring and out. Back then, Iky's nickname was 'Head of Stone.' Iky's Dad had a bunch of T-shirts made up of Mt. Rushmore with Iky's head right in the middle of the four Presidents. Iky's head was even harder than the stone head Presidents.

The people who were working on the Crazy Horse Monument heard about Iky and hired him to work that summer. Halfway into the summer they fired Iky because he was listening to the song 'Running Bear' over the loud speaker. Iky thought Running Bear was running around naked and he was looking for White Cloud toilet paper and he needed some Dove hand soap. Iky was too carried away listening to that song because he was chipping off big chunks of rock with his head. Crazy Horse's nose broke loose and it fell on top of a bulldozer far below. The nose squashed the dozer flatter than day old beer. Luckily, there was nobody in the dozer when the nose went crashing down. They carved out a gigantic rock band-aid over the missing broken nose. Then they started calling Crazy Horse, Chief Flat Face!

Hue Burt was telling Iky about the time when he worked in the Cook Room. There were five strap-off tables and two workers per table. Their job is to fill the empty cages with the glass product that needs to be cooked accordingly in the retorts. Mike, the Lead man told all of them idiots, "There is a group of Corporate women visitors taking a tour through the plant, and you better keep the horse playing down to a minimum." Mike then went to his office, and began filling out the daily paperwork.

Five minutes after Mike had left, those clowns bent one of the workers over a railing and they were pretending that they were giving him bunga-bunga. Hue Burt said, "That is the most ungodly thing that I have ever seen. You jerks look like a wild pack of dogs using up a bitch in heat." Mike finished his paper work, and as he was going back out into the plant, he was looking out of the big hallway windows and saw what was going on.

Mike grabbed the door and ran into the plant. By the time he got back into his department, the group of women were all standing there with there mouths wide open, watching this nature show unfold. Mike was just as shocked as they were. Mike said jokingly, "That's just a part of their job." One woman asked, "How does that have anything to do with somebody's job?" Mike answered jokingly, "They are taking anal probe temperature readings." They called Mike into the office and they wrote him up.

Iky's uncle Ed was quite a character. He was a prankster and a practical joker as well. One of Ed's favorite jokes was; he would whisper very softly, "How do you sell a deaf man a chicken?" Everybody would always ask the same question, "I don't know, how do you sell a deaf man a chicken?" Ed would scream out loudly, "Do you want to buy a chicken?"

Ed decided to pull that joke on Iky, so Ed asked Iky very softly, "How do you sell a deaf man a chicken?" Iky asked, "What?" Ed spoke louder, "How do you sell a deaf man a chicken?" Iky asked again, "What?" Ed yelled, "Do you want, I mean how do you sell a deaf man a chicken?" Iky said, "Well I suppose you scream at the top of your lungs, do you want to buy a chicken!" Ed asked, "Iky how did you know that?" Iky answered, "Because three days ago Alex sold me one of your chickens."

Jimbob Blowme was telling Jerkbob East, "I went to the doctor the other day because my hemorrhoids have been flaring up. Jerkbob asked, "What did the Doc do?" Jimbob answered, "The Doc gave me some of that Preparation H, and I don't like that stuff for two reasons," Jimbob asked, "Why don't you like it?" Jimbob answered, "First, it tastes horrible, and secondly it made my lips shrink so tight, I couldn't eat for three days."

Jimbob Blowme was so ugly when he was born the doctor called in a Proctologist. They flipped a coin and slapped both ends, the doctors began to slap everybody that walked into the room while they were pointing at him and saying, "Are you responsible for that thing?" The hospital made Jimbob's parents take him home and they left him at the zoo.

One night Iky was at Bigfoot's trailer house, and they were really getting plastered. (In other words, they were drunk!) Bigfoot said, "Iky, I almost forgot to tell you that you are supposed to call Mom." Iky walked over to the front door, opened it, and yelled at the top of his lungs, "Mom!" Bigfoot said, "Iky you idiot! Mom is twenty-five miles from here." Iky asked, "Do you think I should use the back door? It's closer." Bigfoot asked, "Why don't you use your cell phone?" Iky answered, "Because I lost it."

Bigfoot said, "I would let you use mine, but it needs charging right now, so go ahead and use my house phone." Iky said, "I don't know Mom's phone number." Bigfoot said, "Look it up in that phone book." Iky spent the next ten minutes looking through the phone book. He put the book down and said, "Mom is not in that phone book." Bigfoot said, "I know that Mom is in the phone book." Iky said, "I'm telling you, I have looked through the M section, and there is no Mom in it."

Iky's psychiatrist shock treatment therapy was a total success; Iky went from a 220 down to an 110. That was very shocking!

Several years ago, Iky took a vacation because his cousin Alex and his wife Kathy came for a visit. They went to Bigfoot's place and while there, they were all drinking. Iky wasn't feeling very good but they went to a catfish restaurant. After they ate, Bigfoot was driving back and Iky said, "Something isn't right, I don't feel good." Alex asked, "What's the matter?" Iky answered, "I don't know, something is wrong." Alex started singing Iky a song, "I think I'm going to die, I think I'm going to die." Iky said, "Shut up and take me to the hospital." They took Iky to the emergency room. The emergency room doctor took Iky's blood pressure and it had sky rocketed. Iky's head felt like it was going to explode.

The hospital staff put Iky in a wheel chair, took him to a room and started giving him shots to bring the blood pressure down. Then they moved Iky in a different room. About ten minutes later, Iky knew that he was going to throw up. He grabbed the closest thing to him, which was a urinal. When he got the urinal up to his mouth, it looked like Mount Vesuvius erupting. The barf went everywhere except in the urinal, because the urinal was upside down. A nurse came in and cleaned Iky up.

The next morning a nurse came into the room and told Iky, "I have a pill that you need to take." She placed the pill on a portable hospital tray. Iky looked at the pill and saw the damn thing was as big as a hotdog. Iky asked, "Where's the hotdog bun that goes with that thing?" The nurse answered, "I am sure we are going to find some buns for it." Iky said, "You might as well get me some mustard too." She said, "I know we are going find some mustard where it's going; now it is time for you to take that pill." Iky yelled, "What are you, crazy? A frickin pelican couldn't even swallow that thing!" At that point, the nurse turned around while putting a rubber glove on her right hand. She said, "Batter up! Now stand up and bend over."

Iky sat there with a blank look on his face. After the nurse shoved Oscar and Meyer up Iky's butt with a broomstick, she left. Iky thought to himself, "After going through that, there is no way that I am ever going to prison." Iky knew then why management personnel and brown-nosers sat on their food. About thirty minutes later Iky thought to himself, "The hell with this shit." He got out of bed and took his I.V. bag with him into the bathroom where he shit the horse pill out. He felt like he had giving birth to a Jerkbob! Then he went back to bed. They called that anal probe injection a suppository; after Iky shit it out, he called it a depository. Iky spent his whole week's vacation in the hospital.

Death's dad Shame won a free ticket to a late night talk show. Shame's seat was located way in the back. The night he was there, the talk show's host was an expert on ghosts and his name was Casper. Casper said, "I would like to have the audience participate in the subject that we are about to discuss. I want everybody in the audience who believes in ghosts to raise your hand." About half the audience raised their hand.

Casper said, "Now, those of you who have raised your hand; how many of you have seen a ghost?" Everybody put their hand down except five people. Casper asked, "Of all you people who have seen a ghost, how many of you have had a sexual encounter with a ghost?" Shame was jumping around as if he has won the lottery, because everybody put their hand down except him. Casper walked back to Shame with his microphone.

Casper asked, "What is your name and where are you from?" Shame said, "My name is Shame Onn, and I am from Pigs Knuckle, Arkansas." Casper said, "Mr. Shame Onn, would you please explain in detail your sexual encounter with a ghost." Shame said, "Ghost? I thought you said a goat." Casper said, "Now shame on you."

One night at work, Big Denny asked Iky "What is the first symptom of aids?" Iky answered, "A hearing disorder." Big Denny said, "No, it's a severe pounding in the ass." Iky said, "I usually get an earache from wearing my hearing aids."

Iky had taken a trip to Russia. While he was in Moscow, Iky's tour guide Boris was showing him around the city. They came upon a scary looking building complex with a twelve-foot high electric fence all around it and bars on all of the windows and doors. There were armed guards with German Shepard dogs patrolling the place. Iky asked, "Is this a Gulag?" Boris answered, "No, this is my apartment."

Iky was cashing his check at the bank and Debbie, the teller asked, "Would you like large bills?" Iky answered, "No bills please, I get enough of them each month at home. I will just take some cash please."

Psycho asked Iky, "Have I ever told you the story about my great-great Grandfather?" Iky answered, "I don't think so." Psycho said,

"Well, my great-great Grandfather was a mercenary. He was in the jungles of the wild Amazons where he was training a rebel army. One day he and two other local soldiers wandered too far from their camp and were captured by a hostile tribe of pygmies. They were taken back to the pygmies' village and brought in front of the Big Chief."

"Everybody in the village came out to watch what was going to happen. Granddad and the two soldiers were kneeling down in front of the Big Chief with their hands tied behind their back. The Big Chief pointed at one soldier and told him to step forward. He was taken before the Big Chief. Big Chief told him he had a choice between bunga-bunga and death. The soldier said he would take bunga-bunga. They pulled his pants down and bent him over. Twenty-five horny pygmies ran out and began using the poor man up. After they had finished, the Big Chief told the soldier he was free to go. They cut him loose; he pulled his pants up and ran into the jungle."

"Then, Big Chief pointed at the other soldier and told him to step forward. He was taken before the Big Chief. Big Chief told him the same; he had a choice between bunga-bunga and death. The second soldier said he would take bunga-bunga. They pulled his pants down and bent him over. This time fifty horny pygmies started using the poor man up. After the pygmies finished bunga-bunga with the second soldier, the Big Chief told him he was free to leave. They cut him loose; he pulled his pants up and ran into the jungle."

"While my Granddad was watching, he was gritting his teeth and becoming very angry. Granddad decided he was not going to take bunga-bunga. The Big Chief pointed at Granddad and told him to step forward. He was lead in front of the Big Chief. Big Chief told him he had a choice between bunga-bunga and death. Granddad looked at Big Chief. He had a big smile on his face. Suddenly my Granddad laughed out in loud defiance and told Big Chief he would take death. Big Chief also began laughing and told my Granddad he would get death by bunga-bunga." Iky said, "Bunga-bunga sounds like a real pain in the ass." Psycho said, "So are hemorrhoids."

Ort was talking to Bigfoot and said, "Did you know that Iky thinks he's an explorer? He believes he has been to he North and South poles since he is Bipolar." Bigfoot said, "Iky also thinks that he's psychic because he predicted the collapse of our economy and many other events that have happened." Ort said, "That is really amazing, how is he able to do that?" Bigfoot answered, "Iky watches the global national news every evening." Ort said, "When you watch the news they tell you what is happening in the world." Bigfoot said, "That's true, but Iky's television set doesn't work."

Iky was having a session with his Psychiatrist and told him, "Doc, I have a very important question for you." The psychiatrist asked, "Well, what is it?" Iky answered, "A question is when you do not know the answer." That was when the Psychiatrist wrote a prescription for a three-month supply of Prozac. Iky asked, "Is that prescription for me?" The Psychiatrist answered, "No, it's for me."

For all of you history buffs, this one may have some interest. During the battle of Britain when England stood alone against Nazi Germany, the Prime Minister of England, Winston Churchill was taking a tour of the bomb-damaged sections of London. He was telling the people how they could take it. An ugly woman came up to him and said, "If you were my husband I would feed you poison." Churchill looked at her and said, "Madam if you were my wife I would take it."

Iky walked up Boris and said, "Boris you are a Homo Sapien."

Boris said, "I'm not a darn faggot."

Back in 1974, Psycho was in the Army, and was stationed at Fort Hood, Texas. That Christmas Psycho took a bus to go back to Fort Smith. Arkansas. When he got on the bus, it was full of soldiers. As he made his way down the aisle, he saw that there was only one seat left in the very back of the bus. Psycho sat down, and the bus drove off. Sitting in the seat next to Psycho was a Mexican.

The poor man was crying and sobbing. He said, "I cannot go home because my family will not understand, boo hoo hoo." Psycho said to him, "It cannot be that bad." The Mexican said, "You do not understand and neither will my family, boo hoo hoo." Psycho said, "I am sure your family will understand. It can't be that bad." The Mexican said, "Nobody can understand what happened to me."

Psycho asked him, "Well, what happened?" The Mexican screamed out, "I just got out of prison, and they made me suck their dicks!" Then everybody on the bus turned around in their seats and was looking at Psycho. Psycho thought that he needed to defuse this situation, so he put his arm around the poor man and asked, "Well, did you get any good at it?"

Iky likes that old saying, "The difference between a wise man and a fool is that a wise man talks because he has something to say, and a fool talks because he has to say something." Nowadays politicians can no longer fool anybody, because politicians make fools of themselves.

Several years ago, Iky's Aunt Winnie, his Mom's sister, came to visit and they went to eat at a Chinese restaurant. After they had finished their meal, Bigfoot asked everybody if they wanted fortune cookies. Iky said he didn't want one. Bigfoot went up to the counter, and got everybody a fortune cookie. Ort read his fortune, "Confucius say man who goes to bed with itchy butt wakes up with stinky fingers." Bigfoot read his, "Confucius say man who stand on toilet is high on pot." Iky could not resist this opportunity so went up and got a cookie. Iky read his fortune, "Confucius say women who fly up side down have big hairy crack up."

Corporate told Flatchest and Nobrains not to attend any more Problem Solving Team Meetings, because the company had enough problems already.

Iky's Psychiatrist decided to try a different approach treating his Bipolar. His doctor had been reading an article on bananas. They are high in protein, potassium, vitamin B6, fiber and many other vitamins that Iky's body was lacking. Doc took Iky off his drug company's synthetic generic pills and placed him on a banana-medicated program. After two weeks Iky went back to see him for a follow up visit. The Doc asked Iky, "How are things going with you?"

Iky answered, "Well Doc, the last two weeks have been very interesting, I have been swinging from trees, I like picking bugs off me and eating them, and I like to pound on my chest and make ape noises." The Psychiatrist looked at Iky and asked, "What are you, bananas?" Iky answered, "There is nothing wrong with me." Iky reached down with one hand and he took a crap in it. Then he threw it at his Psychiatrist. Then Iky sat in his chair making ape noises. The Doc called Debbie his secretary and said, "Bring some bananas, paper towels, a mop bucket, and toilet paper back here right away." Debbie asked over the speakerphone, "Why do you need all of this stuff?" Doc answered, "Because Iky is monkeying around and he just went ape shit."

Terry walked up to Iky at work and asked, "Did you hear about the Pillsbury Dough Boy? Iky asked, "No, what about him?" Terry answered, "He's got doughnuts." Iky asked Terry, "Did you hear what happened to Betty Crocker?" Terry asked, "No, what happened to her?" Iky answered, "She burned her buns."

Terry said, "I also heard that the Pillsbury Dough Boy grabbed Betty Crocker's buns, and she turned around and kicked him right in his doughnuts. Then she filed a sexual harassment law suit against him, and she won a lot of money." Iky said, "Yeah, but I also heard that did not hurt him financially, because the Pillsbury Dough Boy has got a lot of dough."

Around 1900 or so, Teddy Roosevelt was taking a cross-country tour. At one of his stops, he went to a big Indian reservation. He was giving a speech in front of a large crowd of Indians. As Roosevelt was speaking, the Indians were yelling, "Hogwa! Hogwa!" Roosevelt was thinking to himself that they really liked his speech.

After his speech, Roosevelt's Indian tour guide was showing him around the reservation. He showed him their cattle operation, and as he was making his way through the bullpen, Roosevelt almost stepped in a big pile of bullshit. The Indian guide grabbed him by his arm, pulled him back, and said, "Don't step in the Hogwa.

Many years ago, the County Sheriff named Bob was chasing Iky down some old dirt roads in the country. Iky finally pulled his truck off the side of the road. Bob knew Iky and all about his medical condition. As Bob was walking up to the truck he asked, "How are you doing Iky?" Iky answered, "I'm doing just fine Bob." Bob said, "Iky I have been chasing you for the last fifteen miles. Why did you stop here?" Iky answered, "Because I ran out of gas."

Billyjoe Jeffbob's neighbor Hill Billybob is so dumb that, he thinks that an A.T.V. is a television set.

]The company had to send Jerkbob East to rehab for two months because he had a severe drinking problem. The program was a total success. Jerkbob quit drinking out of toilets at bars so that he could get cheap beer. Now the only problem is that Jerkbob has to go back to rehab, because he is smoking out of toilets to get high on pot.

Iky went to the drug store to get some new prescriptions filled. The Pharmacist Don said, "Iky those pills will give you bad gas." Iky said, "That happened to my sister the other day." Don got concerned and worried, he asked, "How is your sister now?" Iky answered, "Well she is doing fine. Why?" Don asked, "Well, what did they do about her bad gas?" Iky answered, "They removed her bad gas and cleaned her out. Then they gave her a refund for the bad gas that they sold her the day before."

Don said, "That is the first time that I have ever heard of a drug company paying for a patient's medical bill because they got bad gas from there medication. Does she have any side effects from the bad gas?" Iky answered, "No, she runs like a dream, and she has even quit smoking." Don said, "That is really amazing that a patient can quit smoking and go out running also. She must have a lot of will power." Iky answered, "No actually, Toot's truck is only two wheel drive."

Iky went to Mc Donald's and drove up to the talking ordering machines. After sitting there for ten minutes and yelling his head off, Iky drove off very angry and upset. The cashier at the check out window saw Iky's truck window was up.

Iky saw his friend Harvey one day at the store; Harvey was walking slow and taking short steps. Iky asked him, "What's the matter?" Harvey answered, "I had a vasectomy yesterday and I am really sore from it." Iky asked, "I'm sorry to hear that. What is a vasectomy, some kind of bug bite?" Harvey answered, "Well sort of. It is when you have your testicles removed." Iky said, "I had a friend of mine who had his removed, and they gave him a lot of ice cream after his operation." Harvey said, "Iky that is tonsillitis. A vasectomy is when they remove your testicles from your balls." Iky said, "That sounds like a pain in the ass." Harvey said, "No, that is hemorrhoids. After you have had a vasectomy you shoot blanks."

Iky said, "I would rather shoot lead." Harvey said, "I don't believe it! Iky you are starting to understand now." Iky said, "Yeah, I like to shoot lead bullets out of my .357 magnum because you cannot hit anything with blanks." Harvey said, "Iky, this is the last time that I am going to explain this to you. A vasectomy is an operation when a male has his reproductive organ removed so he can no longer have children. Now do you understand what a vasectomy is?" Iky said, "I sure do and it takes balls to have a vasectomy."

One night Iky did not get any sleep before he went to work, and he was in a very bad mood. When it was time to send the boil out, Mitch was not at his capper filler. Iky was really pissed off because he got a late start and he was behind schedule. Iky went out to the smoking patio and saw Mitch smoking and bullshitting with the people out there. Mitch saw Iky and said, "My line is hooked up Iky. You can go ahead and run your boil out." Iky looked at Mitch and said, "Bitch, I'm going to take you to the hospital." Mitch asked, "What for?" Iky answered, "I'm going to have them put a plexi-glass plate in your stomach so when

I stick your head up your ass you can see where you are going." Mitch burst out laughing, Iky asked, "What's so funny?" Mitch answered, "My wife told me the same thing."

I am going to have to tell you about Paul Ledge - he looked and sounded just like Popeye. If you tried to have on a conversation with him, you would have to wear a wet suit and have a see through face shield on as well. Talking to him was like standing behind a manure spreader while it was spreading shit. Paul was in an Arkansas National Guard Unit. While he was on duty, he was a cook. One day, his sergeant told Paul to ice down the milk. There were two big tubs; one was full of milk cartons and the other one was full of ice. Paul opened all of the milk cartons, and he dumped the milk over the ice.

During the first Gulf War Paul's unit was on the front lines, and they got orders to move out. Paul jumped in a jeep and took off. Soon he was way ahead of everyone and disappeared. Four days later an Iraqi patrol drove up under a flag of truce. They had brought Paul back. When the Americans interrogated the Iraqis, they said, "We captured this American and took him to our headquarters. We told him that we had ways to make him talk. After thirty-six hours of nonstop mindless babble, we told him that we had ways to make him shut up. This man has the I.Q. of a retarded camel. Three of our best interrogators committed suicide while they were interrogating him and two other ones drowned from his slobber that was flying everywhere."

Iky says, "In order to be a Doctor, you have to have a lot of patients."

Iky's brother Ort is even balder than Iky. One day Ort walked up to Iky and asked, "Hey Iky, what do you think of my new toupee?" Iky answered, "You got a teepee?" Ort said, "No, a toupee." Iky said, "A soufflé." Ort said, "Iky you idiot, I said a Toupee!" Iky said, "Oh, why didn't you say that to begin with? What is a toupee?" Ort answered, "It is an expensive hair piece." Iky said, "Herpes! You got that stuff now too?" Ort yelled, "I said hair piece! A hairpiece is a man's wig! I paid more than five hundred dollars for this thing!"

Iky said, "Man you got ripped off, where is it at?" Ort yelled, "Iky not only are you deaf, but you are also blind! It's on top of my head!" Iky asked, "Is there supposed to be some hair up there, because you look like Bozo the Clown." Ort put his hand on top of his head, and he didn't feel any hair. Ort said, "I know that I put that toupee on my head this morning. It must have fallen off." Iky said, "I know what your problem is." Ort asked, "What's that?" Iky answered, "A problem is an obstacle that gets in your way just like the way you have your soufflé on up side down."

One day at work Iky and Meano were unloading cages on one of the lines. Meano told Iky, "I dated this woman for a while, and I stayed over at her house one night. The next morning when we woke up, there was an ashtray that had a half-smoked cigar in it sitting on her coffee table that was next to the bed." I asked her, "What's with the cigar?" She answered, "I like to smoke cigars."

"I left and went home. She spent the next weekend over at my house. That morning when we got up, she could not find her panties. As we were looking around, I saw them sticking halfway between the waterbed mattress and the frame. I pulled them out and said, "Here they are I found them." She looked at them and said, "Those are not my panties." I said, "Oh, I forgot they are mine. I like to wear women's panties."

Iky and Meano were laughing about that story, and Meano said, "I'm going to go out to the smoking patio and have a cigarette." After Meano had finished his cigarette, he came back laughing. Iky asked, "What's so funny?" Meano answered, "When I was smoking my cigarette I told everyone out there that same story I told you. As I was leaving one of the temporary-workers came up to me and said, "You know, that woman that you were talking about, she is my cousin and she really does smoke cigars."

Iky walked up to Boris at work and said, "Boris, I didn't know that you are a Homo-Erectus." Boris said, "I am not a darn faggot with a hard on."

When Iky was married to Death, he asked her, "How much longer do I have to wait before I can make love to you?" Death answered, "Take a number and wait your turn." Iky said, "I have taken a number and I have been waiting in line for three days. In fact, your Dad is three people ahead of me. I think your mom and your two sisters are behind me, and by the way what's with the midget that's got the two-by-four strapped across his ass?"

Death said, "He's just a friend." Iky said, "Yeah, and what are you doing playing with his peanuts? I suppose he was packing his truck and he is going to move in with you now?" Death said, "He has already moved in." Iky said, Go get me my blindfold, so I don't have to see this." Death said, "I can't do that right now." Iky asked, "Why not?" Death answered, "Because my Dad is going to use it next."

Iky went down to the motor vehicle registration office to renew his driver's license. He took a number and sat down in a chair. After thirty minutes went by his number was called, Iky walked up to the desk and Rose asked, "How can I help you today?" Iky said, "I need to renew my driver's license." Rose said, "It looks like you are going to have to take an eye test." Iky said, "I see." After the test was, completed Rose asked Iky, "Do you have a hearing problem?" Iky asked, "What?" Rose said, "It is obvious that you have a hearing problem." Iky said, "I do not have a hearing problem, I have a people problem."

Rose asked, "I do not understand, what do mean by that?" Iky answered, "Well it is like this. Most people who talk to me do not speak loud enough, so that is their problem not mine." Rose said, "I hear you loud and clear." Iky asked, "What?" Rose said, "I really like you and I am going to give you your new drivers license. Oh, there is another thing I almost forgot to ask. Would you like to be an organ donor?" Iky said, "I'm afraid that I cannot do that." Rose asked, "Well why not?" Iky answered, "Because I don't even have a piano."

When Iky was out on the floor working Hue Burt walked up to him and said, "When I was just a little boy, my Grandmother had some berry bushes growing in her yard. The berries were almost the size of your hand, and they were very juicy." She called them Blossom Berries. Have you ever heard of anything like them Iky?" Iky said, "Yeah, I know what those things are. They call them Dingle Berries." Hue Burt said, "I have never heard of them before." Iky said, "That's those berries that form in the crack of your ass when you wipe your butt with toilet paper." Hue Burt asked, "What do they taste like?" Iky answered, "Shit."

Many years ago, Iky was down in Rochester Minnesota for a boxing fight. When the bell rang for the first round, Iky ran over as fast as he could and caught his opponent still in his corner. Iky knocked him out with just one overhand right. Iky's coach Jim was excited and jumping around.

Jim said, "That was outstanding, I have never seen a more perfect overhand right than that. What made you decide to knock this guy out in his own corner?" Iky answered, "I have diarrhea, and I didn't want him knocking the shit out of me." From that moment on, Jim would give all of his fighters Ex-Lax before they stepped into the ring.

Iky was at a big party and there was a woman sitting there rolling a bunch of marijuana cigarettes. They call these cigarettes joints. She was a very attractive young looking woman. She was wearing really short cut off jeans, and a tank top with no bra that was exposing a large portion of her breast. She looked at Iky and asked," Would you like to try a couple of these hooters?" Iky answered, "Yeah I wouldn't mind doing that, but there are too many people in this room."

This woman was no blond and she took the hint, so she looked Iky over and thought yeah he would do. She said, "Why don't we just blow this joint and go to my apartment? It would be very romantic there." Iky said, "I am really looking forward to that." Iky leaned over the coffee table and blew the joints off onto the floor, and then he said, "Well, I'm ready." She said, "Forget it."

Many years ago when Iky and Roger became friends at work, Roger invited Iky over to his house one weekend for dinner. Iky had never met Roger's first wife, Ada. She cooked a wonderful meal. While they were at the table eating, everybody was quiet. Iky decided to break the ice and spark up a conversation.

Iky looked at Ada and said, "I don't know whether Roger told you or not, but I have aids." Ada whispered softly, "No, he didn't tell me that." Roger was wondering where this conversation was headed. Ada began looking at everything Iky touched or ate off, because when he left she was going to throw everything out. Ada was also going to clean and disinfect the whole house. Iky said, "Yeah, I got hearing aids in both ears."

When Iky was getting ready to start his shift at work, he walked up to the time clock. Terry was standing there looking at a memo posted on the board. It read, "Impact Team Meeting in Dick Monday Room at 4:00pm. Iky looked at it and asked, "Who in their right mind would want to go to the Big Dick Room and get impacted?" Terry said, "Probably people looking for a tight position."

Iky said, "I can see it now. Headline news across the country. Police are investigating a strange and mysterious death in a food plant. Police have not ruled out foul play. An Impacted Team member was found dead yesterday in the Big Dick Room. He was the recording secretary at the time at the time of his death. He was taking bent over excessive amounts of dictation; the deceased pants were pulled down to his ankles. Team members explained the reason that his pants were down. They were giving him mouth to mouth, trying to revive him.

Brown-nosers in space like asteroids.

When Iky was married to Death, one evening they stopped at a pizza place. While they were waiting for their pizza, Death asked Iky, "When we make love do you ever fantasize about other women?" Iky should have said no, that he actually fantasized about being in prison and a big black guy named Bubba was standing behind him giving him bunga-bunga because that is what she was fantasizing about. Why would she ask such a stupid question in the first place?"

Iky was stupid and he said the truth, "Well sometimes I do." Then Death came unglued and yelled, "How could you say something like that! I cannot believe you said that, how could you say that!" Iky said, "The first reason I said that is because you asked me. The second reason why is because you make me wear a blindfold when we make love, and since I cannot see you I might as well be fantasizing about someone else." At that moment, Death shut her black hole, which was her mouth. From then on Iky did not have to wear a blind fold when they made love, and Death would look at Iky to make sure that he kept his eyes open.

Brown-nosers like brown eyes.

Jabo asked Iky, "Hey Iky, what kind of food makes a woman lose her sexual drive?" Iky answered, "Probably anything that they have to cook in the kitchen by themselves." Jabo said, "I like your answer, but it is actually wedding cake." Iky said, "Then don't get married."

Jerkbob East is such a jerk off that his first wife divorced him and remarried not long after. She found herself a much better husband, a real husband that could make her feel like a real woman for a change. She said, "My new husband and I are having the best sex that I have ever had in my life, and I don't have to buy her any Niagara or a dildo like I did for Jerkbob."

Many years ago when Iky lived with his parents up in Minnesota, Iky's Dad had taken a dozer and pushed oak and ash trees into big brush piles. Dad told Iky to take the chainsaw and cut the trees up into firewood. It was the first time Iky had ever used a chainsaw. Iky spent the entire week cutting firewood and Dad drove out to where Iky was working. There were nice neat rows of firewood stacked up everywhere.

Dad asked Iky, "How is the wood cutting going?" Iky answered, "It is going pretty good. I have eight cords of wood cut right now." Dad asked, "Is the chainsaw running all right?" Iky answered, "I guess so, but I think the chain is getting dull." Dad walked over to the chainsaw and he saw that there were no teeth left on the chain. He noticed that there was no bar oil or a gas can around. Dad picked up the chainsaw, and pulled on the cord a couple of times, the chainsaw fired up and it was making a lot of noise. Iky yelled out, "That's the first time I have heard that noise! I wish you had a longer handle on that axe!"

One night at work, Big Denny had finished cleaning the Dry Ingredients Room six hours early. With all of this extra time to spare, he made himself a bed and went to sleep. Ole, his supervisor was out in the plant prowling around. Ole wouldn't go anywhere without his electric buggy. The only reason why he didn't drive his buggy in the office was that it wouldn't fit through the doors. While Denny was upstairs sleeping, suddenly he woke up. Someone was violently kicking his feet. Denny jumped up and he was face to face with Ole. Denny wasn't thinking and he blurted, "Darn Ole, how did you get that buggy up those stairs?"

When Iky was seventeen years old, he took up amateur boxing. His Dad coached him that first year and Dad believed that the training should be tougher than the fights. Dad had Iky put in a whole mile of fence line by himself in just two days. Iky pounded every fence post into the ground with his head.

Management called an emergency meeting about the Meat Stick Department; they were finding too much metal in the product. After several days of brain storming ideas, Management said, "Metal in Meat Sticks is unacceptable." Duh! Management came up with another brainstorm. They rewrote the labels on the jars of the meat sticks. The labels read, "This product contains extra iron for your growing needs." Management had done the same thing years ago back in the Cereal Department when chunks of wood were showing up in the finished product. Management rewrote the labels that read, "This product is also high in fiber."

Gary Man is so lazy they named a recliner after him; they called it the Lazy Boy.

Pamerrhoid Nobrains is so dumb she thinks that Bipolar is two gay polar bears.

Many years ago when Iky's Dad was working in the twin cities, one day after work he stopped at a local tavern. While he was there drinking a beer, there were two men at the bar, and they were telling Polack jokes. The joke telling went on for about ten minutes straight. Finally another man walked up to them and asked, "What's all bloody and screams like hell?" Well, the two joke tellers were sitting there thinking about the punch line. Finally, they asked, "What is all bloody and screams like hell?" The man answered, "The next S.O.B. that tells another Polack joke!"

Jimbob Blowme thinks that a Northern Pike is a toll road in northern Michigan.

The lazy boy Gary Man had learned the facts of life at a very young age. Gary was in the sixth grade, and after school one day he walked into his house. Gary has done this many times in the past, and if he continued to do so, there would be a large hole in the side of the house. After spending the next twenty minutes looking for the front door, Gary finally found the door, opened it, and walked in. Well, it was the entrance to the back cellar. Gary fell twelve feet straight down and landed on top of head. Gary scratched his head and got up as if nothing had even happened. That is just like the old saying, "No brain, and no pain. Or is that no pain, no brain?"

Gary finally walked into the living room. His Dad was sitting in his lazy boy reading the paper. Gary walked up to him and said, "Dad,

I have a question for you." His Dad asked, "Well son, what is your question?" Gary asked, "Dad how come I have the longest dong in school?" His Dad laid his paper down, looked at Gary and said, "Well son it could be the fact that you are twenty one years old." Gary said, "I just turned twenty two yesterday. I have another question for you Dad. The first time that you had sex did it hurt?" His Dad said, "No son, it never hurt."

Gary said, "Dad I had sex the other day with a couple of my school teachers." Gary's Dad got very excited and thought that there might just be some hope for this lazy boy after all, and he asked, "Well son, how did it go?" Usually everybody remembers the first time that, he or she had sex. Gary answered, "Well I know one thing. I really didn't care for it that much." Gary's Dad said, "Aw, just hang in there practice makes perfect. Just like that old saying, a stitch in time saves nine." Gary said, "That old saying may be true. My butt hole sure is sore and bleeding, and I think that if it keeps up like this, I may need nine stitches in time too."

Back in the winter of 1979, it was extremely cold that year. One day Iky and Dad were in the kitchen playing checkers. A little black dog that they had called Grizzly had been missing for about a day and a half. Mom dressed up warmly and took the garbage out side. A little while later the door flies open and Mom is standing there losing her mind. She is hysterical and yelling, "Blah rah rah!" It scared the heck out of Dad and Iky. Dad said, "Calm down, what's going on?" Mom shouts, "Grizzly has got his tongue stuck on the dozer!"

Dad and Iky took a bucket of warm water outside, and sure enough, there's this little dog trying to pull its stuck tongue free from the bulldozer. It's about eighty below out, and this dog has frost all over its head. Its frozen stretched tongue is sticking about ten inches out of the dog's mouth. Dad takes the warm water and pours it slowly over Grizzly's tongue; it frees the dog from the dozer.

They take Grizzly in the house Mom says, "Look at that poor dog." There is Grizzly sitting there looking at us. Grizzly looks like he has a great big shoehorn hanging out of his mouth. Iky said, "Well, look at the bright side." Mom asked, "How could there possibly be any bright side to this?" Dad answered, "You can use that dog for licking postage stamps now." Three days later Grizzly's frozen tongue fell off. They used his tongue for a doorstop.

Jerkbob East is so dumb. He spent a weekend out at his Grandparent's farm. Jerkbob's Granddad told him, "Go out to the barn and milk the goat." Jerkbob milked the Billy Goat, twice!

When Iky was working up on the batch tanks at work, Doris was under the platform cleaning out the steam jets. While Iky went back in the soap room to get some chemicals, Iky's partner Danny filled a stockpot full of cold water, and dumped the stockpot of water on top of Doris while she was down below. Doris let out a scream, and Danny took off running. Doris thought Iky must have done it. That night they had a complimentary dinner for the plant.

When it was lunch break, Iky was in the cafeteria eating his dinner. While everyone was eating and bullshitting, Doris walked in and sat beside Iky. Iky had his bump cap under his chair, so Doris bent down and got Iky's bump cap. Doris turned her back toward Iky and pulled her rubber boots off. She poured the contents out of her boots into Iky's cap. It was brown smelly stinky sewage shit water. It was enough to make a Billy Goat puke. It was enough to gag a faggot I mean a maggot! It was almost as bad as Jerkbob's breath.

Doris put Iky's bump cap back under his chair, then she got up and on the way out, she told everyone, "Watch Iky." Iky looked up at the clock, and saw it was time to go back to work. He reached under his chair, grabbed his cap, and swung it up on top of his head. At that moment, you could have heard a pin drop. Doris burst out laughing; she sounded like a chicken cackling. Iky had shit water running down his head and neck. He got up and ran into the locker room. Iky put his head under the hand washer and was washing his head down with hand soap. He was almost throwing up. The next night Iky walked up to Doris and said, "I owe you an apology." Doris asked, "What for?" Iky answered, "Last night when I dumped that skunk water on my head, the first thing that I thought of was that fuckin bitch!" Doris burst out laughing.

Indian Joe from White Earth Indian Reservation in Minnesota says, "Never eat yellow snow, because it leaves a bad taste in your mouth."

One hot summer day at work Willy McFathead was running the vegetable grinder and Joe was running the meat grinder. Willy went over to Joe and told him to go on break. As Joe was walking away Willy ran up behind him and smeared some meat all over Joe's back. Joe walked up to Iky and said, "Look what Willy just did to me." Iky said, "Joe you are running the meat grinder, and you are also mixing potato flour in with your batches of meat. If that happened to me I would take a scoop of that potato flour and dump it down Willy's britches." Potato flour is some of the nastiest stuff there is. When you add water to it, it becomes a slimy, sticky mess. The dust from this stuff is very irritating because it sticks to anything that is moist.

Later that day, Joe was waiting and watching for the right opportunity. Finally, it presented itself. As Willy was climbing up a ladder to check on his hopper bins, Joe ran over and grabbed the back of Willy's pants and underwear. He pulled it out as far as it would stretch and dumped an oversized scoop of potato flour down Willy's britches. When Willy got to the top of his platform, he was so pissed off that he picked up a rake and threw it at Joe. Joe grabbed a water hose and started soaking Willy down. Willy had great big sticky globs of potato flour falling out of his pants legs! That stuff was so nasty that it glued Willy's butt cheeks together.

One of Iky's coworkers on third shift was Gerald. He was quite a character. Gerald liked to eat baked beans then sit in his bath tube playing with the bubbles that float to the surface. He called that total excitement. That is about as exciting as watching wet paint dry. One night Gerald cleaned up the men's locker room. After he had finished that job, later that same night he cleaned up the cafeteria. Gerald had done a superb job in the cafeteria. He mopped all of the tables with the same mop water with which he had used to mop out the toilets.

Mike says, "The Chinese word for constipation is hung chow."

Iky spent twenty-three years at that factory before he finally became disabled. He had seen five Plant Managers come and go. The plant went down the hill with every new Plant Manager; they were always applying new stupid rules and regulations. The last Plant Manager Iky had was Carol Flatchest. She was so dumb that one day she asked Iky, "What do you think of my new support bra?" Iky answered, "Well Carol that looks really good on you, but there is just two problems." Carol asked, "What are the problems?" Iky answered, "Your support bra is on backwards, and we call that bra a back brace."

Carol Flatchest put a memo up on the board that read, "From now on any employee who is caught farting in the plant will be fired." That was a very bad idea, because from that moment on Management was no longer able to voice their opinions.

One morning while Pamerrhoid Nobrains was in her office, she was hard at work reading the National Enquire. Nobrains phone rang. She answered it and said, "I am busy at this time, and I do not want to be disturbed." It was Carol Flatchest on the line and she said, "Pamerrhoid, this is Carol. I need you to bring me a finger nail file to my office A.S.A.P. (As Soon As Possible) Nobrains said, "Okay Carol, I'm on my way." Five minutes later Pamerrhoid walks into Flatchest's office.

Flatchest was sitting behind her desk; there were stacks of documents on top of the desk. Pamerrhoid said, "I brought you the finger nail file Carol. By the way, what does A.S.A.P. stand for? Flatchest answered, "I'm not sure, but I think it means Always Shout at People. I have the Problem Solving Team working on that one right now." Pamerrhoid asked, "Why do you need a nail file? Do your nails need shaping?" Flatchest answered, "No, Corporate told me to file these documents."

Brown-nosers are Management's best friends because they know all the assholes in town.

Iky's nephew Trenton is in the Air Force. He has been deployed to Iraq and the Mideast four times. One day Trenton asked Iky, "Do you know why the Arabs wear rags on their head's?" Iky said, "I don't know. Maybe they have a headache?" Trenton said, "That's a good guess, but most Westerners don't really know the truth. The Arabs use the rags for toilet paper, because there isn't any toilet paper in the desert. After they wipe their butt with the rags, they stake the rags down out in the sand at night. When they wake in the mornings these shit covered rags are full of dung beetles. The Arabs pick the beetles off the rags, roast them over their campfires, and eat them for breakfast. Then they put the rags back on their heads."

Iky asked, "What do the roasted beetles taste like?" Trenton answered, "Chicken." Iky said in amazement, "No shit." Trenton said, "This isn't the end of the story. One of the Arabs named Omar had been smoking opium all day long, and that night he passed out on the sand outside his tent. Omar was so out of it he didn't take his rag off his head. The next morning his friends could not find him but they noticed their rags didn't have any beetles on them. Momar saw a weird set of tracks leading away from the camp. They followed the tracks for about a mile, and they finally saw Omar. Hundreds of dung beetles had rolled Omar across the desert. Omar's head was completely covered with dung beetles. They woke him up and he told them he had a headache, and asked if it was time for breakfast yet!"

Nobrains thinks that a Polaroid is a polar bear that has hemorrhoids.

Iky thinks that Quarterbacks who play football must be gay. They are always looking for a wide receiver with a good tight end, and they are throwing passes at other men, trying to get at least ten yards.

Iky and Bigfoot drove to their sisters house one day. When they got out of the vehicle, Toots walked out of the house and greeted them, "Hi guys what are you up to?" Iky said, "Oh, about two hundred pounds." Toots asked, "What brings you guys out here?" Bigfoot answered, "Iky's Nissan Xterra. We came to do some fishing in your strip pits, if you don't mind." Toots asked, "Did you guys bring some minnows with you?" Iky answered, "No, but I have worms." Toots said, "Iky, if you want, we can go to the dog kennel, and I can get you medicine for your worms." Bigfoot said, "We don't have time for that."

Iky and Bigfoot went fishing for about five hours. When they finally got back to the house, Toots asked them, "How many fish did you guys catch?" Bigfoot said, "We caught four channel cat." Toots said, "Good! I don't want any cats around my dog kennel. Corey was here fishing last week, and he caught a dog fish." Bigfoot said, "Iky, do you remember that time in Minnesota when I caught one of them?" Iky said, "Yeah, I remember. It was the weirdest looking fish I have ever seen. Toots, what did Corey do with the one he caught?" Toots answered, "He threw it back because it had fleas."

Nobrains thinks that forbidden fruit in the Bible is Fruit of the Loom men's underwear. She also thinks that Adam swallowed a whole apple because he had an Adam's apple.

One night on the graveyard shift, (which reminds me of that joke about undertakers, they occasionally like to have a cold one!) Anyway, one night a bunch of guys were sitting in the locker room bullshitting before their shift began. One of them, a Vietnamese named Hoe Dog, was stretched out on a bench taking a nap. Joe walked in and saw Hoe Dog lying there. Joe unzipped his fly and put his hand inside his pants. He had his index finger sticking out of the zipper. Joe walked over to Hoe Dog and started rubbing his finger on Hoe Dog's lips. Gradually Hoe Dog began to wake up and he saw Joe standing there with what appeared to be his dong sticking right in Hoe Dog's face.

Right then Joe turned sideways, and pulled his hand out of his pants. The fake dong disappeared and he zipped his pants back up. Hoe Dog was furious as he jumped up off the bench. He pulled a knife out and yelled, "If you ever do that again I will cut it off! I mean it, I will cut it off!" He was so angry that he was speaking in Vietnamese. Everybody in the locker room was laughing there ass off. Later Iky walked up to Hoe Dog and said; "Hoe Dog, that reminds me of that old saying." Hoe Dog asked, "What the hell are you talking about?" Iky answered, "The early bird gets the worm."

Management people don't use aspirins, (they pronounce it 'Ass Burns') because it gives them diaper rash!

Iky says, "If you want to be on the same level as Management, all you really need are three things. A septic tank, because they are full of it, a lobotomy because they have no brain, and a twelve pack of beer. That's just in case the lobotomy doesn't work!"

The lazy boy Gary Man has to be the laziest person at work. Let me rephrase that. In this world, his nickname is Jigem Jaws because he spends more time talking about work than actually working. Gary's jawbone muscles are as strong as a jackass is. One day Gary was water skiing and the one hundred and fifty horse powered motor broke down. The motor was pulled off and laid to the side. Gary stuck his head in the water where the motor was and pulled three water skiers with his big ass lips flopping in the water!

Gary's lips were so big that when he talked, Iky told him to quit shouting. They were so big that when he sat in his car everybody thought he had been in an accident because his lips looked like giant air bags! One time the Jaws of Life had to be used to get him out of his car. A bee had stung him on the lips and his lips had swelled so big that if the car's air bag had inflated his head would have exploded.

One cold winter Iky was visiting Alex and his wife Kathy in North Dakota. Kathy looked out the kitchen window and saw Iky sitting outside in a lawn chair, drinking a beer and wearing swimming trunks. It was forty below out with the wind blowing, and there were four-foot snowdrifts in the yard. Kathy yelled to Alex, "Come and look at this." Alex looked out the window and saw Iky. He opened the window and yelled, "Iky, get your butt in the house right now!"

Iky walked into the house and asked, "What do you want? Can't you see that I'm busy?" Alex asked, 'Have you lost your mind?" Iky answered, "Not lately." Alex asked, "What in the hell are you doing out there?" Iky answered, "I'm getting a Yankee tan." Alex asked, "What's that?" Iky answered, "That is when you turn pure white." Alex said, "Well, if you stay out there any longer, you will be frozen." Iky said, "That is a Russian Tan!"

Management had created a very hostile work place. They were totally against drug and alcohol abuse. If they fired everybody at work for these reasons, there would be nobody working at the factory because everybody had to be high or drunk just to deal with the stress and anxiety!

Psycho said, "My neighbor is so fat that whenever her husband wants to make love to her he has to roll her in flour! Then, after she baked for six hours in the sun, he would look for the doughnut!"

Bigfoot's nephew Cave Man was over at Bigfoot's house. While they were playing video games on line, Bigfoot asked Cave Man, "Is little Logan potty trained yet?" Cave Man answered, "Yes he is, but it took us a while to train him. Logan doesn't even use diapers anymore." Bigfoot said, "Well hey, that's great!" Cave Man said, "Not really." Bigfoot asked, "What do you mean by that?" Cave Man answered, "Because now whenever Logan has to go, he craps and pisses on the floor." Bigfoot said, "That reminds me of that old movie." Cave man asked, "What movie was that?" Bigfoot answered, "Logan's run."

Back in Minnesota in the winter of 1975, Little Iky and Little Bigfoot were outside digging snow tunnels that were part of a snow fort. They had constructed a snow tunnel that was at least thirty yards long. In the middle of the tunnel, a shaft extended seven feet straight up. This was an entrance located in the middle of a big snow mound. Both of the ends on the main shaft were open so they could be used as exits or entrances.

Iky was outside playing with a deer hide and using it as a snow sled. He climbed up on top of the snow fort, placed the deer hide over the top entrance shaft, and sat down on top of the deer hide. Bigfoot had crawled into one of the side entrances and he realized he was standing right beneath Iky. There was a rope on the deer hide that was dangling from the shaft above.

Bigfoot looked up and saw the rope, and he pulled on it with all of his might. Suddenly, the deer hide slid halfway down into the shaft and became stuck. Bigfoot could hear a high-pitched blood-curling scream, which he had never heard before and was sure he would never hear again. Sitting on the deer hide, Iky was bent like a horseshoe; his arms and legs were sticking straight up past his head, and he could see his own stomach. His neck was about to break, and he couldn't even move.

Iky was letting out a blood curdling, high-pitched scream. Bigfoot tried to free Iky but he could barely move because he was laughing his ass off. Iky knew that he was going to die. After what seemed to be an eternity, Iky finally fell through the shaft. Iky yelled at Bigfoot, "Why didn't you help me?" Bigfoot answered, "I tried to, but I couldn't move because I was laughing too hard!"

Before moving to a trailer, Iky and Bigfoot used to live in an apartment. One Saturday morning when Iky got home from work, he walked into the bathroom and saw Bigfoot lying on the floor unconscious. Bigfoot had been out bar hopping the night before and had drunk himself to death. With Iky's quick thinking, he saved Bigfoot's life. After Bigfoot came to Iky explained to him what had happened. Iky had to revive him and saved Bigfoot's life. Bigfoot said, "Man Iky, if you hadn't given me mouth to mouth resuscitation, I probably would have died." Iky said, "I didn't give you mouth to mouth." Bigfoot asked, "Well, how did you revive me?" Iky answered, "I ran next door and borrowed the neighbor's dirty toilet bowl plunger and used that instead, By the way, you need to go take it back."

Bigfoot said, "He's a poet and didn't even know it, and his feet are Longfellow's."

Jerkbob East's wife is so fat that if she had been on the Titanic during its maiden voyage she would have sank the iceberg!"

During hunting season, Sonny was out at Ft. Chaffee deer hunting, and he was in his stand before daybreak. Off to the left he heard whooping, hollering, and yelling going on. Sonny wondered what in the world all of that commotion was. Then he saw that there was an Indian standing out in the middle of a cold creek.

The Indian was reaching down with both hands, and throwing ice-cold water up on top of his head and onto the back of his neck. The Indian was cussing up a storm, hollering and yelling while doing this. Sonny asked the Indian what had happened. The Indian told him that he had pulled his coveralls down to his ankles and taken a crap. After he had finished he pulled the coveralls back up, the hood flopped up on his head, and it was full of shit! He had taken a crap inside the hood!"

One Saturday morning Toots and Mom drove over to Bigfoot's trailer house. It was about twelve o-clock as they walked onto the front porch. Toots starts knocking on the door. Bigfoot was still sleeping and didn't come to the door, so Toots walked over to the bedroom window and started banging on the wall. Boom! Boom! Boom! Boom! It was shaking the whole side of the trailer house. Bigfoot jumped out of bed extremely pissed off. Right at that moment the window shade flipped up and Bigfoot was standing there stark ass naked.

Bigfoot looked out the window and saw on the porch next door a family was having a barbeque cook out. A little boy saw Bigfoot and said, "Look, there's a naked man." Then everybody looked over and saw Bigfoot. He was fumbling with the shade and finally got it pulled down. Bigfoot put on a pair of pants, ran to the front door and opened it. Toots and Mom were standing there. Bigfoot said, "If you weren't my sister I would kick your butt!" While Toots was laughing, she said, "Hey Bigfoot, if you want women to go out with you, you need to change that birthday suit."

Jerkbob East is so dumb that he thinks that a model T is a plastic doll that looks like Mr. T.

As Iky was checking out Hanging Judge Parkers Museum in Fort Smith, Arkansas, he went outside to look at the hanging gallows. There was a Park Ranger there and he told Iky, "Back in those days, one of the famous outlaws was Cherokee Bill. They finally caught and brought him before Judge Parker." The judge told Cherokee Bill, "They will hang you from your neck until you are dead, dead, dead. Do you have any last words?" Cherokee Bill replied, "Yes Judge, I do. You can kiss my ass until it's red, red, red." Iky said, "I didn't know that Hanging Judge Parker was an ass kisser." The Park Ranger said, "He wasn't. He was an ass kicker."

Bigfoot was over at Iky's house and they were watching a D.V.D. Bigfoot asked, "How long is this movie?" Iky answered, "Oh, about six inches."

One night at work while some of the people were playing poker in the break room, Crack Shack asked, "What do you call a flea on top of Iky's head?" Nobody could figure that one out, so Crack Shack answered, "Homeless."

Pamerrhoid Nobrains was talking to Carol Flatchest and she said, "I'll be glad when this day is over. When I get home I'm going to take a long, hot shower." Flatchest said, "You can't do that today."

Nobrains looked very puzzled and asked, "Well, why can't I take a shower today?" Flatchest answered, "Because the weatherman said no showers for today."

One winter day when Iky was in grade school, a bunch of kids were outside on the playground during the first lunch break. One kid named Craig Havercamp (his nickname was Haverpampers,) had made a snowman and was very proud of it. The school bell rang, signaling the start of the second lunch break. All of the kids ran back inside except Haverpampers. He didn't go back in right away, because he was guarding his snowman. About five kids from the second lunch break were looking at Haverpampers snowman, standing and waiting like a bunch of vultures.

Haverpampers was begging them to leave his snowman alone. He finally left and went back into the school building. Later that day Haverpampers went out to the playground, and when he saw his snowman, he started crying. His snowman had been assaulted and destroyed. The hall woman saw him crying, so she walked up to him and asked, "What's the matter, Craig?" Haverpampers cried, "They wrecked my snowman, boo hoo hoo!" The hall woman said, "Everything is going to be all right."

She put her arms around him and gave him a big hug. Haverpampers head was on her chest as he was sniveling and crying. He pulled his head back. There was a great big glob of frozen snot on the hall woman's chest, still attached to Haverpampers nose. It looked like an ice bridge for the ice road truckers. Haverpampers tried to brush off the frozen snot. From that moment on, the hall woman's nickname was Snotgrass.

One day, when Hue Burt was in his work area a couple of maintenance men drove up in a buggy parked it and went to lunch. After their lunch break was over, they climbed back into their buggy. Hue Burt decided to run up behind the buggy and slowly pick the rear end up so that the back wheels weren't touching the ground. The driver turned on the buggy and stepped on the gas pedal. The back wheels began spinning but the buggy went nowhere. The driver put it in reverse, and still nothing happened but the back wheels were spinning.

The driver was so frustrated that he started turning the key on and off, changing the gears from forward to reverse repeatedly. In one final act of desperation, he jammed the shifter forward and slammed his foot down on the gas pedal. At that moment, Hue Burt let go of the buggy and it took off like a rocket. The rear end of the buggy fish tailed from side to side. The driver had no control of the buggy as it crashed into the wall. The buggy was totaled. The driver was drug tested and passed the drug test. Management ruled the accident was due to mechanical failure.

One cold winter in Minnesota Iky and Bigfoot were out in the barn goofing around taking turns riding on one of the cows. After a while, the cow sat down and wouldn't move. While Bigfoot was sitting on the cow, Iky saw a pair of old fashioned sheep shears hanging on the wall. Iky took the sheep shears and poked the cow in the butt. The cow got up, started bucking and jumping around, but after a while got used to it, and stopped moving.

Well, the two morons traded places so Iky was sitting on top of the cow. Bigfoot started poking the cow with the sheep shears but still, the cow didn't move an inch. Bigfoot stood there scratching his head, assessing the situation. He heard a cat meowing, looked down and saw it rubbing on his legs. Bigfoot grabbed the cat by the back legs and swung the cat up and over the cows butt.

As soon as the cat's claws made contact, Bigfoot pulled the cat towards him. The cat's claws began digging in just like a farmers plow busting up a field. The cow lost its mind and started mooing frantically. The cow went berserk. It bucked Iky up in the air and took off running. Iky landed on his butt on top of a frozen cow pie. While he was lying moaning in pain and suffering from brain damage, Bigfoot said, "Hey

Iky that was fun! Do you want to try it again?" From that moment on, we could never ride that cow again.

Iky's family moved from North Dakota to Minnesota. That fall when school started, Iky's two brothers and sister had to ride bus number 13 for one week, and then they switched over to bus number 17. Bus 13 picked up the kids around the Strawberry Lake area who were a bunch of mean country kids. When Iky got on the bus that morning for the first day of school, he found a seat close to the back of the bus.

There was a big mean girl sitting behind Iky. She turned the ring that she was wearing around so that the emerald was in the palm of her hand. She began to slap Iky on top of his head with the ring. Iky didn't do anything so she just kept hitting Iky over and over. While she was hitting him, Iky's mouth was filling up with spit.

Iky couldn't hold anymore spit, and he thought to himself, "If she hits me just one more time that's it." Well, she hit him again and Iky spun around and spit right in her face. Her face looked like the foamy flowing Colorado River. Her mascara and make up were running down her face like a mud side. That was the last time she ever hit Iky.

Iky likes that old saying that he has incorporated for his illness. "If you want to find sympathy for Manic-Depression, just look it up in the dictionary. It's between shit and syphilis."

When Bigfoot and Iky lived back at home in Minnesota, their parents had bought a brand new stove and refrigerator. Bigfoot and Iky took the boxes that these items came in out to the barn. They cut a couple of eyeholes in each box so that when they got inside they could see where they were going. The cow was in the barn, so Iky and Bigfoot started making weird ass noises, and began ramming the cow with the boxes.

The cow totally freaked out. It knocked Bigfoot over, and was jumping up and down on him while he was in the box. Bigfoot was screaming and finally the cow ran off. Iky helped Bigfoot out of the crushed box; Bigfoot was all battered and bruised. Iky said, "Hey that looked like fun! Do you want to do that again?" Bigfoot moaned, "Cowabunga."

One morning the graveyard shift was waiting at the time clock getting ready to go home. Dave started doing his ape impression. He walked from side to side, and swung his arms back and forth. He was also making loud ape noises. Also standing at the time clock was a group of temporary workers. Dave walked up to one of the older women, and while still putting on his ape impression, he put his arm around her.

Everybody was laughing their butt off when suddenly Dave disappeared. John saw Dave sitting over at the banana machine by himself with a blank look on his face. Dave was very depressed. John and Iky walked over to him. John asked, "Dave, what's the matter? Are you alright?" Dave answered, "You know that woman that I just put my arm around?" John asked "Yeah, what about her?" Dave answered, "She told me that she is horny on Fridays." Iky said, "Hey man, this is Friday! Cheer up Dave; this is your lucky day. Take her home with you and give her a banana!"

Iky's friend Killer told him a story about when he was in the Air Force. Killer had a friend named Joe. Joe would walk around the base picking up every piece of paper that he could find. He would look it over and say, "That's not it." Then he would drop the paper and move on. Everybody started getting really worried about him. Joe was sent to the base psychiatrist. After he had a thorough evaluation, Joe received his discharge papers. As he walked out of the building, Joe looked at the paper in his hand and said, "Now that's the paper that I've been looking for!"

Many years ago, Iky and Bigfoot went over to Ort's house. They were all in the hot tube getting gooned up. Bigfoot started getting rowdy and threatened to whip Iky and Ort's ass. Iky said, "I think that we're going to have to work him over." Bigfoot said, "I've been drinking whiskey!" Bigfoot took a swing at Iky. Iky ducked the punch, and he hit Bigfoot in the stomach with a right hand uppercut. While Bigfoot was gasping for air, Iky shoved his head down in the water. As Iky was holding Bigfoot's head down, weird looking debris floated to the surface. Iky saw it and he pulled Bigfoot's head out of the water. Iky asked, "What are you doing, chewing Copenhagen?" Ort saw the wreckage floating in the hot tube, and he yelled, "He just puked in my hot tub!" They all bailed out of the tub, and that was the last time Iky or Bigfoot were allowed in Ort's hot tub again.

One morning at work, the R.F.G. (Restrained and Finished Goods,) department was getting ready to have their morning meeting. The conference room for that department was up above their office. While everybody was waiting on the staircase that took you up to the meeting room, Skully was talking to Hue Burt. They didn't notice that the supervisor had opened the door and the crowd of people was moving up the staircase. Hue Burt saw the gap in the crowd and he said, "Come on Skully, the line is moving."

Skully turned around and started walking up the staircase. Skully tripped on one of the steps, and while he was falling, he was trying to grab anything in arms reach to break his fall. He looked like a cat trying to claw its way out of a tow sack, Skully reached out and grabbed Don's left leg on the way down; Skully ripped Don's leg right off. Most people didn't even know that Don had an artificial leg. Some of the people were freaking out including Skully. While Don was hopping around on one leg, Skully was lying on the staircase in shock holding Dons leg. Hue Burt said, "Skully quit pulling Don's leg and give it back to him. I want to get some coffee and doughnuts."

One of the teams called Braggers and Boasters decided they needed to build up the declining moral in the plant. A day was set aside for a free lunch, and a raffle drawing was held for the employees. As usual, the only employees that won any door prizes were the Brownnosers. When Jerkbob East's name was drawn, he was jumping around in excitement. Jerkbob thought that he had won a brand new toothbrush. About a week went by and Jerkbob was talking to Jimbob Blowme.

Blowme asked, "Well Jerkbob, how do you like the door prize you won?" Jerkbob answered, "I'm glad that I won it, but I still don't have it broke in yet. The bristles on it are just too stiff." Blowme said, "I'll trade you the one I have at home. We have been using it for three years now, and it is broke in. They swapped brushes and after a week, they met in the hallway at work. Blowme asked, "Do you like that brush that I traded you Jerkbob?" Jerkbob answered, "I sure do, and your toothbrush doesn't make my gums bleed like that new one did." Blowme said, "That thing is a toothbrush? How stupid of us! We were using ours as a toilet bowl brush."

As Iky was getting ready to go home from work one morning, he changed back into his street clothes. When he put his boots on, Iky noticed that on one foot was his work boot, and on the other was his cowboy boot. Iky was in a hurry because he didn't want anybody to see his boots. As he was making his way out of the plant, there were two office people sitting behind a desk in the main hallway. When Iky walked up along side of them, a woman said something to Iky. He didn't hear what she said so he stopped and asked, "What?" She asked, "Would you like to sign up for the awards banquet?" Iky looked at her and answered, "No thank you that is against my religion." Iky turned around and he walked out the door.

Years ago, Iky's family would spend Thanksgiving at Uncle Ed and Aunt Elaine's place. Elaine and Iky's mom were sisters; Ed and Elaine were Alex's parents. One Thanksgiving, Bigfoot and Iky found this really neat toy rifle. It had some cool features, there was a grenade launcher on it that shot out grenades, and it made realistic gun shot noises when you squeezed the trigger.

Iky and Bigfoot started arguing and bickering as to who was going to play with the gun. It got to the point where it almost turned into a fistfight. Alex got tired of listening to the two morons bickering, so he stepped in between them. Alex grabbed the gun from Bigfoot and he said, "Follow me." They went to the shop where Alex laid the gun down on the ground. He took an axe and chopped the rifle in half. He handed Bigfoot a half and Iky the other. Alex said, "There you go now shut up!" Iky said, "I want the other half."

The Plant Manager, Carol Flatchest was having a butt-chewing meeting with a group of supervisors. As she was pacing the room back and fourth, Flatchest had a memo in her hand. Flatchest said, "This memo says that many of the employees are abusing their breaks. You need to put a stop to this, because only I can abuse these breaks!" She crumpled the memo up in her hand, and threw it on the floor. Flatchest started pacing back and fourth, tripped over the memo, and fell down.

A supervisor yelled, "That looks like down time!" Another one yelled, "That looks like a safety hazard!" A third one yelled, "Is this meeting over now?" Flatchest yelled out, "No, this meeting is not over yet, safety is not an issue, and as for the down time situation, production is what I want; production at all cost." Flatchest got up off the floor and started pacing the room again. Flatchest pounded her fist on the table and yelled, "I will not stand for these issues anymore!" Someone yelled out, "Then sit down!"

When Psycho was in grade school, he heard some of the kids talking about a penis. When he got home from school, he asked his Dad, "Dad, what is a penis?" Psycho's Dad said, "Follow me son." They went into the bathroom where Psycho's Dad whipped out his penis and said, "Now son, this is a penis; you can't get any better than this. This one is perfect." Psycho looked it over and said, "Okay Dad." The next day at school a girl came up to Psycho and asked, "What is a penis?" Psycho answered, "Follow me." They went behind the school and Psycho pulled his penis out and said, "Now, this is a penis; it would be perfect if it was two inches shorter." The girl said, "If it was two inches shorter there would be nothing there."

When Iky was married to his first wife Death, he heard that old saying, "One mans loss is another mans gain." After they got divorced, Iky said, "One mans loss is another mans pain." If a twenty-ton nuclear bomb exploded right beside Iky, he would yell out, "I want more pain. This is child's play after living with Death!"

When Iky and Bigfoot were kids, they were out in the shop playing around. The big rollup door was down and there were hundreds of flies around the windows on the door. Iky got the vacuum cleaner and they started sucking up the flies. After a while, they wondered what they were going to do with the flies. Bigfoot looked over and saw a propane tank, Bigfoot said, "I have an idea; we will gas those flies." They took the vacuum cleaner over to the propane tank. Bigfoot turned the tank on and the gas was hissing out. Iky sucked up the vapors with the vacuum hose.

This vacuum cleaner dated back to the 50s; it was a silver cylinder rocket looking contraption. On the back end of the vacuum cleaner, it looked just like a modern day jet engine. When it was running there were sparks shooting out of the back. As they continued sucking up the vapors, a spark ignited the gas inside the vacuum cleaner. All of a sudden, there was a tremendous explosion. The vacuum cleaner flew about seven feet straight up in the air and then crashed back down onto the concrete. It looked like it was snowing in the shop, because of the dust falling from the ceiling. Iky unplugged the vacuum cleaner, and Bigfoot turned off the propane. They hurriedly put the vacuum cleaner back, and from that moment on their Dad could never figure out why the vacuum cleaner was full of dead flies, and why it would not work!

Jimbob Blowme thinks that the Polar Ice Caps are the warm stocking caps that the Green Bay Packer fans wear at their football games.

Iky says, "Do you know what is dumber than credit cards? People who are dumb enough to use them." Uncle Ed told Iky once, "A Jew does not brag on how much money he has spent, he brags on how much money he has saved." Iky can't figure out the credit card concept. Credit card companies encourage you to get their credit cards so you can establish credit. In reality, you are going into debt, but they call that credit, and when you can't pay off your credit cards, then they call that being in debt. If you do not want to go in debt, than don't get any credit cards."

Jimbob Blowme and Jerkbob East were recently driving around the city park. They were enjoying one of their favorite past times - picking up gay men. Jerkbob said to Jimbob, "Pull into the restroom. I have to go." Jimbob drove to the restroom. Jerkbob got out of the truck and went in the restroom. Jerkbob came back out and said, "There's no toilet paper in there." Jimbob said, "Well, use a dollar."

Jerkbob went back into the restroom. After five minutes, Jerkbob came out with shit all over his hands. Jimbob asked, "What in the world happened to you? I told you to use a dollar." Jerkbob answered, "I did use a dollar, see?" Jerkbob held out his shit covered hand with two dimes, a nickel, and two quarters in it. Jimbob said, "That's only seventy five cents!" Jerkbob said, "Give me a nickel so I can go back and finish!"

The Company hired a janitorial service to clean the offices, break rooms, hallways, and locker rooms. The people would come in on the graveyard shift. One night a woman was in the men's locker room cleaning. She set a sign up outside that said, "Janitor working." No one was supposed to go in while she was working. Boris had to take a leak. As he walked into the locker room, he saw the sign, but he couldn't read or write.

While Boris was using one of the urinals, he looked off to his right. There was the cleaning woman looking at Boris, her mouth wide open. She was in shock because Boris's meat stick was huge. To her it looked like an elephant's trunk sucking up water. Boris looked at her and shouted an old Alabama love poem to her; "Get on your knees bitch!" She ran screaming out of the locker room, which is why Boris's nickname is Big Bore.

When Bigfoot moved to Fort Smith, Arkansas back in 1978, he had a 1967 Ford Mustang. One night he was out partying with one of his friends. They stayed out all night until all of the bars closed. While Bigfoot was taking his friend home, he was hot rodding around town, His friend would say, "Turn here." Bigfoot would turn the steering wheel sharp, and the wheels would make a loud screeching noise. After several more turns like that, Bigfoot missed the last turn. He slammed on the brakes, shifted into reverse, and floored it. All of a sudden, there was a loud crash.

Bigfoot looked in the rear view mirror and saw lights flashing. The rear end of the Mustang was on top of the hood of a cop car. Bigfoot looked out his window, and there was a cop standing looking at him. The cop asked Bigfoot, "Are you in a hurry?" The cop told Bigfoot's friend to go home. Bigfoot went to jail and he got a D.W.I. When Bigfoot went down to his insurance company, the secretary asked him, "Were you the one who totaled that cop car?" Bigfoot answered, "Yeah that was me." She started laughing and said, "Well at least you didn't have to call a cop." Bigfoot said, "Yeah. But I had to call a Bail Bondsman."

Ort and Roger were over at Iky's house one day. Ort was bragging about all of the nice fish that he had caught two days ago in the Arkansas River. Roger asked Ort, "Well. Haven't you heard what's been going on lately?" Ort asked, "No, what?" Roger answered, "The Fort Smith sewage treatment plant has been broken down, and for the last week and a half they have been pumping raw sewage into the river. Iky said, "Hey Ort, next time you go fishing there again, just take some used condoms and fill them up with shit." Roger said, "Yeah, that way you can do some condom fishing." Iky said, "Hey Ort, did you know that master bait is used to catch large fish?" When Ort got home, he threw out all of his fish in the freezer. I guess they left a bad taste in his mouth, because they psychologically tasted like shit.

The first four days weren't so bad when Iky was in the hospital because his blood pressure had gone haywire until Iky's roommate went home. Iky's new roommate was a ninety two year old man. They wheeled him in on a wheelchair, and then put him in the bed next to Iky. The night with the old man started out like this. Iky would be on the verge of falling asleep when suddenly, the old man started yelling at the top of his lungs, "Nurse, Nurse I'm dying, I'm dying!" Iky sat up in bed, and about that time, a nurse came in the room. She talked to the old man for a little while then she left.

Iky lay back down, and started to fall back asleep, and then, "Nurse, Nurse I'm dying, I'm dying!" yelled the old man. At first, Iky was worried and felt sorry for the old man, but as time began to drag on, Iky's blood pressure began to climb, because now the nurse's were ignoring the old man. He was still screaming bloody murder; Nurse, Nurse I'm dying, I'm dying!" Iky pushed his bedside button; a nurse walked into the room and asked Iky, "Can I help you?" Iky yelled, "Can't you hear that? It's not me! He needs help; he's dying!" The Nurse said, "All of the Doctors have gone home, and he will see a doctor in the morning."

Iky was on the verge of losing it. He started looking at his pillow, and then he looked at the old man. The old fart was just like the Energizer Bunny. He just kept yelling and yelling. Iky was almost to the point of yelling, "Shut up you dumb bastard, of course you're dying, what the hell do you expect, you're are ninety two years old!" As morning arrived, a Nurse brought Iky some breakfast. All of a sudden, Iky started to smell something. The smell gradually started intensifying to the point that a Turkey Vulture wearing a gas mask would have puked twice. After a while, there were three nurses in the room.

As they were sitting the Old Man up in bed, the sheets on the bed were stuck to his back. The Old Man had been shitting all night, and this brown looking gravy, super glue substance made the sheets stick to his back. As they began to peel the sheet off his back and the smell began to intensify horribly, a Nurse came in and apologized to Iky. She said, "I am sorry about this, if you want, we can bring you some more breakfast." Iky said, "What good would that do me, when I can't even eat this shit that's in front of me. Oh, and by the way, there is just one more thing, Nurse. I'm dying, I'm dying!" The Old Man shouted, "That S.O.B. has been screaming that all night long!"

As Pamerrhoid Nobrains was walking down the hall at work, she passed the bulletin board, and something caught her eye. It was a memo written by the Plant Manager, Carol Flatchest. The memo read, "Due to a conflict of interest, the plant will no longer be hiring relatives." Nobrains panicked! She and Jimbob Blowme got a divorce. She thought by doing that her and Blowme could still keep there jobs. But they are still legally brother and sister.

Iky stopped at his Mom's house. Mom said, "I am so glad that you are here, I have been looking all day long for my car keys and I can not find them. Iky said, "Mom, I know where your keys are at." Mom asked, "Well, where are they?" Iky answered, "They are in your right hand." Mom said, "Oh! I feel so stupid. I have one more problem." Iky asked, "Well, what is your problem?" Mom answered, "Can you help me find the car?" Iky answered, "No problem Mom, we are sitting in it right now."

The Jocks at work who go down to the gym to workout are so lazy they pay other people to workout for them.

Just recently, several former Presidents and their wives got together for a dinner party. After they had many rounds of stiff drinks, Jimmy Carter said, "The hardest thing about my term in office was trying to get my reforms passed through congress." George Bush Jr. said, "The hardest thing about my term was trying to remember my lines for my speeches." After thinking for a while Bill Clinton said, "The only thing that was hard during my term in office was that thing between my legs." Hillary said, "I wouldn't know anything about that." Rosalyn Carter said, "We know." Laura Bush said, "We heard that Bill has quit playing his saxophone, and now he likes to play with his whoremonica."

Bigfoot was in high school taking gym class. After class was over, everybody went into the locker room to take a shower. One of the jocks was named Steinke and he was walking around with a pissed off look on his face. He was holding his street shirt in his hand. Someone had taken his shirt and wiped their ass with it. From that moment, Stinky Steinke had a shitty outlook on life.

One day Iky walked into a bar and he sat down drinking a beer. After having many rounds, Iky was getting gooned up. A man walked into the bar and he sat down drinking a beer. Iky looked at him and there was a toad sitting on top of his right shoulder. Iky walked over to the man and asked, "Where did that thing come from?" The toad answered, "First it started out as a pimple on my ass." Iky said, "It looks more like a hemorrhoid to me."

Jerkbob East said to Jimbob Blowme, "I gotta go take a shit." He went to the restroom, and after ten minutes came back. Blowme told him, "I have to take one too." When Blowme came back, he was holding a plastic bag. Blowme asked Jerkbob, "What do you do with this shit after you have taken it?" Jerkbob answered, "I usually put it in my locker, and then I take it home with me."

Roger and his second wife Pam were driving around town. As they were passing a house, there was a person bent over working in a flowerbed. Roger looked at that and said, "That sure is a good looking ass." Pam said, "But that's a guy." Roger said, "Yeah, but it still looks good."

Several years ago, one of the women at work was interested in Iky. Iky would flirt around with her, but that was as far as it would go. Iky always said, "The only dangerous thing about a married woman is her husband." After a while, she went around the block with everybody at work. Out of curiosity, Iky asked his friend Clay, "What was she like?" Clay answered, "The best way to describe her is she was the next best thing to jacking off." Iky said, "She must have been pretty good then."

While Bigfoot was sitting in a bar drinking a beer, there was a man on his left side drinking a coke. The front door opened and another man walked in, and he was looking the place over. The man had a nametag with Jack written on it. He walked up to Bigfoot and asked him, "Are you with that guy?" Bigfoot looked at him and answered

"No." Jack walked over to the man sitting on the bar stool next to Bigfoot. He hauled off and knocked him off the stool.

While the man was lying on the floor out cold, Jack was still hammering on his head. After he had finished whipping the man's butt, he walked out. The bartender was in the back so he didn't see what happened. When he came back out front, he saw the man lying on the floor out cold. He asked Bigfoot, "What happened to that guy?" Bigfoot answered, "I don't know. But I don't want what he's been drinking, because it looks like Jack and coke will knock you out."

Meano told Iky, "Beauty is only skin deep." Iky asked, "Yeah, but what if you are a hippo?"

Spangler the Mangler was telling Iky, "My parents have ten rent houses. A big fat woman lived in one of the rent houses. Two months went by and she never paid the rent. She moved out and trashed the place. There was garbage everywhere. I went into the bedroom, and saw that she had pushed two beds together. When I pulled the beds apart, I heard a loud thud; something fell to the floor. There lying on the floor was a gigantic carrot with a rubber glove on it." Iky said, "She must have been giving herself a five finger discount. What did you do with the carrot?" Mangler answered, "I gave it to Jerkbob and he ate it." Iky said, "Well, at least the rubber glove protected the carrot." Mangler said, "Yeah but he ate that too."

Iky says, "Nowadays when you go to the grocery store, the only thing you end up taking home with you is the receipt, and that is if you're lucky."

Mitch the Bitch was at work one day, and he had the unfortunate luck to see an older woman named Marge approaching him. She walked up to Mitch and lifted her shirt up past her boobs; she was not wearing a bra. Marge shook her shoulders from side to side. Mitch told Iky, "It looked like two monkeys in a tow sack fucking." Iky said to Mitch, "Better you than me."

Iky was talking to Don the Pharmacist. Don said, "Benjamin Franklin said if a house guest stays for more than three days, they start smelling like fish." Iky said, "If they stay longer than a week, they smell like rotten fish."

When Iky was a sophomore in high school Bigfoot was a senior. Bigfoot's friend Tom was Lip's brother. At lunch break after everyone had finished eating, Tom was standing out in the hall talking to Bigfoot. He had a big cupcake called a snowball. It had white glazed coconut frosting around it, and was cream filled. Tom started taking it out of the wrapper, and as he began to take a bite, Iky came running over doing a flying leap. Iky smeared the snowball in Tom's face, and took off running. Tom was chasing Iky and told him, "Iky, I'm going to kill you."

Iky ran around the corner, opened a door and ran through the gymnasium. The door closed behind Iky. When Tom came around the corner, he grabbed a different set of doors. He jerked the door open. There was a chain running through the door and it was padlocked to another door. The chain swung the second door out and it hit Tom right in his head. He was really pissed off now. Iky spent the next ten minutes running and hiding from him. When Iky started to sneak around a corner, Tom grabbed him and smeared the snowball in Iky's face. Iky went into the restroom to clean up. Leroy saw Iky and asked, "What happened to you?" Iky answered, "I just got snowballed." Leroy said, "But there isn't any snow outside, this is May."

Iky told his Mom, "I heard the other day a woman went to a liquor store, and she had bought two cases of beer. A checker carried the beer out to her car for her. She opened the back door on the car, the man threw the two cases of beer in, and they landed on her baby that was in the back seat. Mom said, "That is terrible." Iky said, "The baby is alright, because it was light beer." Mom said, "If it was regular beer that might have hurt."

Iky's friend Jim said, "My ex wife drove me to drinking." Iky said, "Well, that was nice of her to drive you to the bars." Jim said, "Not really, because she left me there."

Several years ago whenever Bigfoot would go to work in the mornings, he would stop at McDonalds and get a large coffee to go. Bigfoot would drink his coffee while he would weld. Back then, the coffee cups were Styrofoam. After Bigfoot had finished his coffee one morning, he got a brainstorm. Bigfoot took the empty cup and turned it upside down. He took an acetylene torch and turned on the gas. Bigfoot held the cup above the torch and filled the cup up with gas. He then sat the cup upside down on a steel table that was a quarter inch thick.

Bigfoot lit the torch and put the lit torch on the cup. There was an earth shattering Ka Boom! The whole shop shook. It looked like it was snowing. Little white pieces of Styrofoam were floating down from the ceiling along with the dust off the steel beams. The table had a great big dent in the middle of it. The whole work crew ran over to Bigfoot asking him, "What in the hell happened?" Bigfoot answered, "I put too much cream in my coffee."

Iky and Roger were having a hypothetical conversation about the benefits of working out and staying in shape. Working out will not guarantee that you will live longer, but it may help you live healthier. Roger said, "Iky, I just want you to know that if you ever become a paraplegic I will take care of you. I will put you on a high protein diet." Iky said, "Well, thank you Roger." Iky sat there for about thirty seconds thinking of the true meaning of what Roger had just said. Then Iky looked at Roger and said, "Up yours."

The company that Iky worked for had its main plant located in Michigan, Jerkbob East and Jimbob Blowme went to Michigan for one week during the winter for a management-training program.

The training program consisted of teaching them to improve their harassment tactics on the other employee's in the plant. Harassing the senior employees was beneficial because if any employee reported that they were being harassed by these two bullies, the employee was told they could lose their job. Many senior people quit out of frustration, and they lost all of their benefits. This created a huge turnover in the plant, and it was cheaper to hire new employees.

A big shot named Allen was conducting the meeting in Michigan. He decided to take Blowme and Jerkbob ice fishing. Allen thought he would show these two Southerners what Yankee ice fishing consists of. The company had several fish houses out on a lake. Allen took Jerkbob and Blowme to a fish house and said, "Everything you need is in that fish house. I'm going to a different fish house and I will be back in six hours." After six hours had gone by Allen walked into the fish house and asked, "Well, how many fish have you guys caught?" Blowme answered, "None." Allen looked and saw something floating in the fish holes. Jerkbob asked, "Oh, by the way, the toilets are backed up. How do you flush them?"

Iky walked up to his Shop Stewart Harvey and said, "I want to file a grievance." Harvey said. "Okay, what is your grievance?" Iky answered, "My grievance is against the Human Resources Director, Pamerrhoid Nobrains. In order to be a Human Resources Director, don't you have to be human first?" After Harvey wrote up the grievance, everybody in the plant signed it.

Iky's neighbor Goosie told Iky, "There are two things guaranteed in this world, death and taxes." Iky said, "I know, I am being taxed to death."

Iky said to Psycho, "Women are the root of all evil." Psycho said, "That's supposed to be money is the root of all evil." Iky asked, "Have you ever seen women save any money like the way I have?"

Iky's friend Jabo told him, "This woman walked into a liquor store, and while she was up at the counter, the cashier grabbed her and started kissing and licking all over her body. She freaked out and ran out the door. A little while later, she came back in with a cop. The cop talked to the cashier, and then he told the woman that she couldn't press charges against the man. She asked the cop why she couldn't press charges. The cop told her it was because he had a lick her license."

Iky can't figure out that medicine men take that gives them an erection. On the box, it states, "If you have an erection for more than eight hours call your doctor." Iky says, "The heck with the doctor, start calling up old girlfriends."

Whenever Pamerrhoid Nobrains and Carol Flatchest use vibrators, they always wear mouthpieces. That way, they do not chip their teeth.

Back in 1975, Ort was home on leave from the Army. Iky and Bigfoot decided to show him what they had been doing when he was gone. They had taken a bicycle inner tube and cut it in two pieces. They tied a knot on one end of each half of tube and put sand inside them. The sand was about eight inches up from the knot. So, Bigfoot and Iky put on a show for Ort. They started battling each other with their homemade black jacks. They were swinging the tubes and hitting each other with them. Ort was standing there laughing his butt off, and he said, "Let me try that."

Iky handed Ort his weapon. Ort was standing there with a big smile on his face. Bigfoot decided to swing his weapon behind him and as he started to swing it back around, he took a step forward. The inner tube stretched out about five feet; it crashed into the side of Ort's jaw, and spun his head sideways. When Ort turned his head back around, there was no smile on his face, and his face was beet red. If looks could have killed, Bigfoot would be dead right now. Now Bigfoot had fear in his face, so he took off running. While Ort was running him down, he gave Bigfoot a double drop kick whammy in his ass. Bigfoot fell down in pain, and Ort was beating the tar out of him with the bicycle tube. While all of this was going on Iky was laughing his butt off, and thinking about that old aftershave commercial Skin Bracer. Their motto was, "There is nothing like a cool slap in the face!"

While Iky was waiting in a check out line at the store, the manager noticed there was nobody waiting on him. There was a group of churchwomen behind Iky, and they were all wearing dresses. The manager yelled out, "Checker on aisle six." A minute went by and the manager looked over at aisle six. Iky was going from one woman to the next, lifting their dresses up, sticking his head under, and feeling around.

The manager ran over to Iky and yelled, "Have you lost your mind?" Iky said, "Not lately." The manager began apologizing to the women, and then he said to Iky, "Do you know that you can get into a lot of trouble for doing that?" Iky said, "Hey chill out, I did what you told me to do. You said check her on aisle six, so that's what I was doing." One of the women said to the manager, "Leave him alone and let him finish his job. Besides it is my turn next."

Bigfoot told Iky, "School was the most downgrading thing that I had to go though in my life." Iky said, "That's because your grades were not up."

Iky was walking along a beach and he found a magic lamp. When he rubbed it, a Genie appeared before him and said, "I am the Genie of the lamp, and I will grant you three wishes." Iky laughed and said, "You sound just like a politician, like John McCain or Barak Obama." The Genie said, "I will guarantee you your wishes, because I am an Independent. Corporations do not tell me what to do or say." Iky laughed and said, "An Independent will never win, you have to be either a Democrat or a Republican." Iky dropped the lamp and walked away.

Jerkbob East is so dumb that every time he goes out into the plant, there is always an earplug dangling from the rear end of his pants. It's because whenever he reads the package that says earplugs, Iky wrote on all of the packages rear plugs.

While Iky was talking to his Uncle Dennis on the phone. Dennis asked, "Iky, what is it like when you are having a manic episode?" Iky answered, "You have your highs and your lows; one minute you feel like you are God and you can solve all of mankind's problems. It can all change in a heartbeat because the next minute everything is a conspiracy. People are out to get you because you know too much." Dennis said, "That sounds just like George Bush. I'll bet you he is Bipolar too."

Psycho was shopping in a store one day, and he saw Pamerrhoid Nobrains pushing a cart. She had her baby grandson with her. While Psycho was talking to her, he started smelling a terrible odor. Psycho looked at the baby, and the baby had shit running out of his diaper. Psycho said, "Pamerrhoid, you need to change that baby's diaper." Nobrains said, "The box said it would hold up to thirty pounds." Psycho said, "They are talking about the box, not the diaper." Nobrains went home and duck taped the box to the baby's butt.

Iky said to Bigfoot, "I got some love gas for you." Than he let out a great big fart. Bigfoot said, "I want a divorce."

Maryjane said to Iky, "I have been constipated all day." Iky said "No shit, look at the two bright sides." Maryjane asked, "How can there possibly be any bright side to constipation?" Iky answered, "First, you save on toilet paper, and second, would you rather have diarrhea?"

One morning while Iky was making breakfast, Maryjane was getting ready to go to work. The local news was on the television. Maryjane walked into the kitchen and said, "The news was talking about when the founding fathers wrote the constitution, they said that, no idiot or insane person would be allowed to vote. Congress is trying to pass a law that will overturn this law." Iky said, "It's the Democrats and Republicans trying to change that law." Maryjane asked, "How do you figure that?" Iky answered, "Because you would have to be an idiot or an insane person to vote for a Democrat or a Republican."

Vinnie the Moocher at work is so cheap. Whenever he gets breakfast in the cafeteria at work, he puts about six pieces of bacon on his plate first, and then breaks up a couple of biscuits. He then takes the broken up biscuits, and puts them on top of the bacon along with some gravy. That way he does not have to pay for the bacon. Talk about bringing home the bacon! Moocher has a big nose because air is free. They banned Moocher from playing poker at work, because whenever he owes you money he says, "Credit." You probably wouldn't even want to get a magnet that is stuck to metal from him, because it would bounce.

When Alex and Eddie's Mom Elian died, Iky was at the funeral. Elian was Iky's aunt on his Mom's side. After the funeral, there was a poker game at Alex's house. All of Alex's cousins on his Dad's side were there. After several rounds of card playing and heavy drinking Iky asked, "Can anybody break a hundred for me?" Alex answered, "I can." Iky handed Alex a one hundred dollar bill. Alex took the bill and tore it in half, then handed the two halves back to Iky. Iky almost became unglued, but he should have known better. Years before Alex would take a deck of cards and say, "Who wants to play fifty two cards pick up?" If you said you wanted to play, Alex would throw the cards up in the air, then say, "There you go! Now pick them up." Anyway, back to the poker game. Alex said, "You can break a twenty the same way." Iky said, "You do that again and I will break your head."

Iky's Dad Raymond was born in 1933, six years before World War II began. All across the country, everybody was bringing in scrap metal. They used the scrap metal for the war effort. The main purpose of the scrap drives was that it helped unite the country. There were posters hanging up everywhere that said, "Give us your scrap and slap a Jap." Everything that you could think of was used as scrap metal - civil war cannons, church bells, sewing machines, cars, pots and pans, kerosene lamps, farm equipment, and the list went on.

Dad would load his wagon up with scrap metal, and then take it to Rogers, North Dakota. The scrap metal dealer would weigh Dad's metal, and then he would be paid so much a pound. Dad would always show up just a few minutes before the scrap dealer would close up and go home. After Dad got his money for his scrap, he would go to the local diner and get an ice cream cone. When Dad finished eating his ice cream cone, he would take his wagon back to the scrap metal dealer and load up his wagon with the scrap that he had just sold to the man. Dad would pull his wagon of scrap back to his house, and a couple of days later he would pull his loaded down wagon back to the scrap dealer and he would be paid again.

Napoleon Bonaparte said, "Religion is what keeps the poor from murdering the rich." Today, bunga-bunga in prisons keeps the poor from murdering the rich.

Meano asked Iky, "Why do Arkies go to movie theaters in groups of eighteen or more?" Iky answered, "I don't know. Maybe it takes that many Arkies to figure out where the theater is at?" Meano answered, "No, the sign says under seventeen not admitted."

Jerkbob East last diet was a total failure. He put on so much weight afterwards. He made Fat Albert look skinny. While Iky was taking a leak in the urinal, Jerkbob walked in and used a urinal next to Iky. Iky looked over at Jerkbob and said, "Gosh darn, you're fat! I'll bet you can't even see your dong. Why don't you diet?" Jerkbob asked, "Well, what color is it now?" Iky answered, "I don't know. I do not have a microscope."

Several years ago Iky, Bigfoot and Joe had bought tickets for a Super Cross motorcycle race in Oklahoma City. These were the top riders in the country. The night before the race, Iky came down with the flu. The next morning Iky almost decided to stay home, but then he thought, "I paid good money for this ticket, so I'm going to go." Well, they took off for Oklahoma City. When they got there, they stopped at a restaurant to get something to eat. They walked in, sat down, and looked at the menu. The server asked them what they wanted to drink. Joe and Bigfoot ordered a coke and Iky ordered a large iced tea. When she came back she brought their drinks, and then they placed their orders.

Iky chugalugged a couple of big gulps of his iced tea. Right at that moment Iky's stomach felt like it had a nuclear bomb exploding inside it. The gases were building up at an alarming rate. Iky said, "Boy, my stomach sure fills upset." He stood up and ran to the restroom. Iky barely made it in time. He dropped his pants, and stuck his butt on the toilet seat. There was a loud "Thhhhh Splat Thhhhh Splat Splat

Thhhhh." This went on over and over. The gases in Iky's stomach were pushing the liquefied shit out so hard and fast that as soon as it hit the water the shit was bouncing right back up onto Iky's butt. There should have been a squeegee hanging on the door, because that was what Iky really needed. Just when Iky thought he was finished it would start all over again. "Thhhhh Splat Thhhhh Splat Splat Thhhhh."

After Iky finally finished wiping his butt cheeks, he stood up and pulled his pants up. Iky flushed the toilet, and while he was washing his hands, he heard running water. He turned around and the toilet was overflowing just like a brown Niagara Falls. Iky ran back out to his table. While he was sitting there eating, about twenty-five G.I.'s walk in and sit down. Iky was watching them. One of them got up and made a beeline to the restroom. Iky started laughing and Bigfoot asked, "What's so funny?" Iky answered, "Watch that G.I." No sooner than the G.I. went into the restroom, he came out even faster. Bigfoot looked at Iky and said, "You made the toilet overflow, didn't you." Iky said, "I didn't do it, it was the two rolls of toilet paper that did it."

Iky was out cutting firewood. When he got back to the house Maryjane was getting ready to go to work. Iky could tell that she was upset about something, Iky asked, "What's the matter?" Maryjane answered," I was watching my soap opera, when all of a sudden Barak Obama cut into the show. He was giving a speech about his new economic plan and how his newly appointed team members will straighten up this country. While he was giving his speech, he had a Bush moment." Iky asked, "What is a Bush moment? Was he drinking a beer?" Maryjane answered, "No, he could not remember some of the lines in his speech." Iky said, "Maybe Obama has the same speech writer that George Bush has!"

Iky thinks that Crow Magnum is three-inch shotgun shells used to shoot crows.

Iky was talking to Bigfoot and he said, "I can not stand those lazy scumbags at work. They won't do their jobs, and someone else always has to pull their load. The people who do work are the ones that are being used up, because the more work you do the more work they dump on you and that just burns my ass." Bigfoot asked, "Do you know what burns my ass?" Iky asked, "No, what?" Bigfoot stands up and he raised his hand up above his waist and said, "Flames up to here."

One night at work Meat Loaf the Lead Man walked up to Harvey and said, "I want you to go relieve Iky for break." Harvey asked, "Where is Iky working at?" Meat Loaf answered, "He is in the break room playing dominoes, and those guys want you to take his place because he doesn't know how to play."

At the start of Abraham Lincoln's presidency in 1861, the first thing he did was fire the Secretary of War, Simon Cameron. Lincoln said, "Cameron was so corrupt the only thing that he would not steal was a red hot stove." Iky feels the same way about this big CEO's. They are asking our government to help bail them out. They have taken what John F. Kennedy said in his speech and turned everything around. Kennedy said, "Ask not what your country can do for you, but what you can do for your country." The CEO's say, "What can my country do for me because I'm not going to do anything for my country." W. Durant said, "A great civilization is not conquered from without until it has destroyed itself from within." Franklin Delano Roosevelt said, "When it comes to politics, nothing happens by chance - it was planned that way." Finally, yet importantly, Fred G. Sanford said, "I am all for capital punishment. I believe everybody in the Capital ought to be punished." Especially for getting our country into the mess that it is in today.

Right before Iky married Death he thought; there was something wrong with the woman. Like the time when they stopped a restaurant to get some breakfast. While they were sitting there looking out the window, Death said, "There's my Daddy pulling into the parking lot. I wonder what he is doing here. He is supposed to be at work. I wonder if he is having an affair with one of these waitresses." Iky asked, "Which One?" Death answered, "All of them." Just like the old saying, "Like Father like daughter."

There is an old saying for couples who tie the knot. They call it the ball and chain. Death had Iky's balls so wrapped up in a chain that she was strangling the poor bastard to death. Iky could not go anywhere in public with her without her accusing him of looking at other women.

Well, what did she want him to do? Look at other men as she was doing? It got to the point to where Iky could not even watch television at home, because there were women on the boob tube. She would have made a blind man put the blindfold on his Seeing Eye dog and accuse him of looking at other women.

Recently Jimbob Blowme and Jerkbob East went to the new movie theater that just opened up in town. The actors who played in the movie were nothing but a bunch of assholes. The movie was an action packed love story. Jerkbob and Blowme even cried during the movie. The name of the movie was "Anal Rampage." They had a gay old time at that movie theater.

Psycho said to Iky, "There are a lot of people who feel that this new administration is going to try to mess with the second amendment of the constitution. That clearly states, we as American citizens have the right to keep and bear arms." Iky asked, "Do you remember when we worked at the plant? What they did to Mike Bear?" Psycho asked, "No, what did they do to him?" Iky answered, "Mike works out at home, and he believes in no pain no gain so he gets results. Mike always used to wear short-sleeved shirts at work. One day he was called into the office, and management told him he could no longer wear short-sleeved shirts out in the plant because his bulging muscles intimidated people. From then on Mike wore long sleeved shirts. The plant took away his right to keep and bare arms." Psycho said, "That has got to be one of the dumbest things that I have ever heard. What were they afraid of, that if Mike flexed his muscle it would make an earthquake?" Iky said, "I hope the government doesn't try to take our short sleeved shirts away from us, because we have the right to keep and bare arms."

When Iky moved down to Arkansas back in 1980, he and Bigfoot were sharing an apartment. Iky bought a pair of boxing gloves at a local pawnshop and planned to teach Bigfoot how to box so he could have a sparring partner. So Iky showed Bigfoot how to hold his hands, how to move his feet, and some basic one two-punch combinations to work on. Iky was going to bring him along very slowly. They put the gloves on. Iky began throwing lazy jabs. Bigfoot timed it and came up and over with a jackhammer right hand that crashed into Iky's jaw. Iky hit the floor.

That was the hardest punch anyone had ever hit him with. While Iky was on all fours trying to shake the cobwebs out of his head, he was seeing stars and little green men. Iky glanced up and saw Bigfoot hopping up and down like a bunny rabbit, with a big grin from ear to ear. Bigfoot stood there hitting his gloves together. While Iky was looking up at him, Iky thought, "Okay, I'm going to teach you a lesson." Iky jumped up, stepped forward, and hit Bigfoot with four machinegun left jabs with power behind every one of the punches. Blood was flying out of Bigfoot's nose. His face looked just like a speed bag being punched. Bigfoot pulled his gloves off and through them on the floor. He said, "I quit." That was the last time that Bigfoot ever put the gloves on with Iky.

The lazy boy Gary Man has the biggest set of lips in the world. The best way to describe them is if you saw a four hundred pound naked woman on a nude beach who had diarrhea, her butt cheeks look just like Gary's lips. All he ever did was talk shit anyway. When he gets chapped lips, Gary uses fifty-five gallon barrels of industrial strength Chap Stick.

Iky walked into a store carrying a box of Depends. He demanded that they give him his money back. A woman from the returns department asked Iky, "Why do you want your money back?" Iky opened the box up. He reached inside the box and pulled out a shit dripping smelly diaper. The woman yelled, "How dare you bring that thing in here? You are supposed to throw that thing away after you have finished using it! Were you born in a barn?" Iky looked at her and answered, "First of all, I don't know where I was born, because I don't remember. Secondly, yes I do know that you are supposed to throw them away after you are finished with them. Thirdly, that shit smelling diaper was already in the box when I bought it. Some asshole had already used it!" Iky borrowed one of Rodney Dangerfield's famous one-liners; Iky looked at the woman and said, "You are an inspiration for twin beds."

When Iky was around twelve years old he had a little toy helicopter called a Vertibird. It could fly around and hovers just like the real thing. At the time Iky's archenemy was his sister Toots. She was mean to him from the day he was born. One of her favorite things to do to Iky was stick her tongue out at him and Iky the double finger whammy. She would always make sure that nobody saw her doing this. One time Toots knocked Iky down on the floor. She got on top of him and forced Iky's shoulders down with her knees. Then she began to slap Iky in the face repeatedly, all the while laughing at him.

One time when she gave Iky the tongue double finger whammy, Iky got so pissed off so he charged her. Toots picked up a frying pan and every time she hit Iky on the head, it was followed by a swift kick. Talk about scrabbled eggs. The last time Toots pulled that stunt on Iky, he was walking into the kitchen, and she was there giving Iky the tongue double finger whammy again. Iky said, "If you do that to me again, I'm going to knock your block off." Well, she did it again, Iky ran over to her and Toots spun him around, and was choking him. Iky broke loose, he hit her with a right hand punch, and there was a loud smacking noise. Both of Toot's lips were bleeding, and she was bawling her head off. Mom came running into the kitchen and she screamed at Iky, "You get out of this house!" Iky was trying to explain to her what had happened, but Mom didn't want to hear it. Iky had hurt her little innocent darling daughter. As Iky was walking out the door he yelled out, "Say hello to hot lips for me!"

Ort and Bigfoot were out bailing hay. Iky told them what had just happened. They were both laughing there asses off. Bigfoot said, "I'll bet you that she is going to destroy your Vertibird." Iky said, "If she does I'll kill her." When Dad got home from work, there was no discussion at the supper table about what had happened that day. Later on that evening Iky walked into his bedroom, and there lying on the floor was the Vertibird destroyed. There were broken pieces scattered all over the floor.

Iky knew that if he punched Toots again, he might get in trouble, so Iky picked up some of the pieces. He walked into the living room bawling his head off, and he said, "She destroyed my Vertibird!" Dad picked Toots up with one hand, and he was beating her ass with the other one. While this was going on Iky was really laughing, he was just faking that he was crying. From then on that was the turning point. Iky would occasionally go into Toot's bedroom, and take one of her teacups. Iky would take a leak in the cup and he would pour the pee all over her pillow. Then Iky would turn the pillow upside down. That was not teatime; it was pee time. Iky called that stuff Minnesota fabric softener. Just like the old saying, "When it rains it pours." That was the last time that Toots ever gave Iky the tongue double finger whammy, because she got a double whammy herself that day. That is just like the old saying, "Don't get mad, get even."

Iky told Tommy, "Management suffers from constipation of the brain and diarrhea of the mouth." Tommy said, "No shit."

Jimbob Blowme was very excited when he won the Arkansas State Million Dollar Lottery. Jerkbob said, "That is awesome Jimbob. Just think, now you are a millionaire." Jimbob said, "I still can't believe I won it." Jerkbob asked, "Well, what are you going to do? Take a lump some payment, or are you going take like thirty year payments?" Jimbob answered, "Well, I talked it over with Nobrains because she knows more about this financial stuff than I do. So I did what she suggested to do." Jerkbob asked, "Well what are you going to do?" Jimbob answered, "To pay less taxes on it, I'm going to get one dollar a year for a million years." Jerkbob asked, "Can I get a loan?" Jimbob answered, "Sure, just wait a hundred thousand years from now." Jerkbob said, "I can't wait!"

The factory that Iky used work for had created such a hostile work environment. All personnel in management had applied for and received gun permits. The security guards were also armed. However, after two weeks, they disarmed the security guards. Management was pissing off the guards worse than the employees at the plant.

When gas was up to about four dollars gallon, Iky saw a woman pushing a car into the gas station. Her husband was behind the wheel. Iky ran over and helped her push the car up to the gas pump. Her husband got out of the car and walked up to the gas attendant to pay for the gas. The woman said to Iky, "Thank you for helping me, I am exhausted." Iky asked, "How far did you push this car by yourself?" The woman answered, "About four miles." Right then her husband walked up and said, "Here is your pack of cigarettes honey." Then he looked at Iky and asked, "Can you help her push the car home?" Iky answered, "Sure, I need a smoke break first." The woman asked Iky, "Can I bum a smoke?"

When Iky and Bigfoot were kids, they were out in the yard playing around. They were playing demolition derby on there bicycles. They were ramming each other trying to knock the each other over. Toots walked out and she wanted to play too, so she got on her bike. While her and Bigfoot were battling each other, Iky made a great big circle and as he was coming back around. He was peddling as fast as he could go. He plowed right into the left side of Toot's bike. He knocked Toots and her bike over, and Iky took off peddling away. Toots jumped up and started chasing and yelling at Iky, "You S.O.B.! I'm going to kill you!" Toots finally caught up to Iky, and she grabbed the back of the seat. She was shaking the bike trying to knock it over. Well that didn't work and she was really pissed off. Toots pushed with all of her might on the back of the seat. Iky was peddling ninety miles an hour and she stopped chasing him. Iky yelled out, "Hey thanks for the push! I didn't know that I was a S.O.B., I guess you must be my mother!"

Psycho was telling Iky, "I can't believe the price of everything nowadays. Now I have to buy my needs, not my wants. I haven't bought any Viagra in several months." Iky jokingly said, "I know what works just as good, and it doesn't cost that much money." Psycho asked, "Well, what is it?" Iky answered, "That Miracle Grow plant food." As funny as it sounds that stuff really works, because Psycho is walking around with a gigantic, not an organic green thumb. If the Jolly Green Giant saw it, he would cry.

Many years ago, Eugene's second wife Mary Jo Bendover became pregnant. She went around telling everybody that it was a miracle baby. Well, I guess miracles do happen, especially since Eugene had a vasectomy when he was married to his first wife, and they had no kids.

Iky figured he better have a man-to-man talk with Eugene. Eugene said, "Iky, I am really excited about this new baby." Iky said, "Well, I'm really happy for you Eugene. How many kids do you plan on having?" Eugene answered, "Well, I haven't really thought about that." Iky thought about it and he was no dumbass.

As time went on tragedy struck. Mary Jo had a miscarriage at an abortion clinic. Now what are the odds that she just happened to be driving by an abortion clinic when she had her miscarriage? Eugene was devastated about it. Eugene's best friend Long Dong was also shook up about it too. Not long after that, Long Dong went down to the clinic and had a vasectomy too. Now if you had seen Long Dong's wife, you would ask, "Why would he need a vasectomy after looking at that?"

Long Dong and his wife have been married for twenty-five years and they had one child that was not even Long Dong's child. Now you know why they never had two. Well, Mary Jo never had another miracle baby after that, and Eugene could never figure out why. Long Dong was always buying that Miracle Grow stuff, and Mary Jo was always going out to the movies, two or three time's a week with her best friend. Just like the old saying, "What are best friends for?" There is an old expression not used any more for that situation, Eugene got, "Long Cocked." I guess Eugene's problem is that he just doesn't have balls anymore.

Bigfoot was talking to Iky and he said, "I don't think that our government should bail out the big three." Iky said, "I didn't know our government was going to bail out Roosevelt, Churchill, and Stalin. I thought those guys were dead. That must be the lend lease act they are talking about." Bigfoot said, "No Iky, they are talking about bailing out the big three auto makers because they are all broke." Iky said, "I don't think that our government should pay their bail. They ought to let them crooks rot in jail."

Bigfoot said, "If our government bails them out it is really nothing more than black mail." Iky asked, "What black man? What does a black man have to do with this?" Bigfoot answered, "Black mail is a form of revenge, just like these big CEO's are saying, "If you don't help us out, it will be your fault that we will go bankrupt." Iky said, "One reason why the big CEO's are going bankrupt is because they have their money in corrupt banks. Besides, I have never had anyone try to black mail me because I usually get white mail in my mail box."

One day at work, Vinnie the Moocher was going to pull a joke on a Q.C. (Quality Control) woman. Moocher was inside one of the empty cages that they cook the jars of food in. Some people put a plastic divider over the top of Moocher. Then they put some jars of cook product on top of the divider. Moocher was balancing the divider, and he could see up through the divider because there were small holes in it. Then they pushed the loaded cage up to the Q.C. station. Whenever they start running product, the Q.C. woman always takes about five jars out of the first cage she runs tests on the product ready for market. Moocher was sitting inside the cage, waiting like a trap door spider. As the Q.C. woman reached out to pick up the sample jars, Moocher jumped out of the cage. He was going to grab her shoulders, but he grabbed both of her boobs instead. Moocher let out a louder scream than she did! Who scared who?"

A long time ago Bigfoot was at bar, and he had drank way too much beer. The bartender took his keys away from him and called Bigfoot a cab. The cabdriver and bartender both had to help Bigfoot get into the back of the cab. The bartender gave the cabdriver the directions to Bigfoot's house. While they were on the road going to Bigfoot's house, Bigfoot asked, "Hey Buddy, do you have room for a pot of oyster stew, and a box of crackers up front?" The cabdriver answered, "I sure do." Right then Bigfoot turned around, and he stuck his bare butt over the top of the seat. It looked like an oil well gushing out oyster stew and crackers. The cabdriver pulled over and said, "I can't believe my luck. Last night a guy asked me if I had room for a pizza and a case of beer up front, and then he puked all over me." Bigfoot said, "That was my brother Iky."

When Iky was just a little kid growing up in Minnesota, one winter Ort and Bigfoot had walked down to the pond to do some ice-skating.

As Iky was walking down to them, Ort yelled out, "Iky bring the scoop shovel." Iky couldn't hear what he said so he said, "What?" Ort yelled louder, "Iky bring the scoop shovel!" Iky said, "What?" Ort started to lose it. Ort and Bigfoot were both yelling, "Iky, bring the scoop shovel!" Iky said, "What? I can't hear what you're saying."

Every time Iky would say what, he would walk about twenty yards closer to them. Iky was about thirty-five yards from them, Ort had totally lost it, and he yelled one last time, "Iky, bring the scoop shovel!" Iky said, "What!" Then Ort and Bigfoot started chasing Iky back up to the house, and they were both yelling, "Iky, we are going to kill you!" Iky was scared to death so he climbed up a tree. Ort and Bigfoot started bombarding Iky with snowballs. Iky asked, "What were you guys yelling about? I couldn't hear you." Ort yelled, "We said bring the scoop shovel!" Iky said, "Well, since you're up here why don't you get it yourself?

Death always kept hounding Iky that they needed credit cards. The only way that Death could get any credit cards was if Iky would co sign for her and he wouldn't do it. Death asked, "What's the difference if you have ten thousand dollars in the bank, and I have ten thousand charged up in credit cards? Iky answered, "Oh, about twenty thousand dollars." Death asked, "How do you figure that?" Iky answered, "Most people can figure that up with a calculator. It would cost me at least that much money to pay off your credit card debt plus interest with my money, if you didn't go bankrupt first." Death yelled, "My Daddy went bankrupt and he got back on his feet!" Iky said, "Yeah, and that bankrupt loser Shame has got stinky athletes feet."

Many years ago in a planet far away; aw, that is just a good beginning for a story. Anyway Uncle Ed, Alex, Bigfoot and Iky were driving around town, and Bigfoot said, "Toot's new boyfriend Jim is coming over tonight for supper." Then, crazy Ed rolled down his window, stuck his head out, and yelled at people on the street, "Big Jim's coming! Big Jim's coming!" Everybody was laughing their ass off. And the funny thing is, I have finally realized the punch line to what Ed was saying. That is almost like asking, "Do you know what comes in quarts?" Answer, "An elephant." Get it.

Iky was born with major hearing loss. As he was growing up Iky took six years of speech therapy, because he could not pronounce the vowels or syllables correctly. The kids in school used to call him slobber jaws because the spit and slobber would fly out of his mouth whenever he would try to talk to you. If Iky had not taken speech therapy, he would have got a job working for the forest service. Iky could have walked up to a forest fire and put it out just by talking.

One morning Iky and Maryjane drove over to Ralph and Willa's place. As they were pulling into the yard, they saw Ralph outside playing with his grandson, Taylor. Taylor was making a construction site out of sand. He had many kinds of toy earth moving equipment. Taylor had constructed roads and bridges, and right in the middle of the site was a great big mound of sand. When Iky and Maryjane got out of the vehicle, Taylor ran up and said, "Iky and Maryjane! Come over here! I have something to show you."

While they were looking at the site Taylor asked, "What do you think of this?" They both answered, "Taylor that is a work of art, you have done a really good job." Taylor said, "Thank you, I have to go get Buddy now." So Taylor ran to the house. Ralph said, "I do this every morning with him, and Taylor is a very smart kid." Right then Buddy, their little house dog ran up. Buddy was checking out Taylor's work of art. Buddy walked right in the middle of the construction site, raised his hind leg, and pissed on the mound of sand.

While they were standing there laughing Iky said, "I guess Buddy was just marking his territory." Ralph said, "No he wasn't doing that." Right then Taylor ran up and asked, "Well Grandpa, did Buddy like that one?" Ralph answered, "No Taylor. Buddy didn't like that one either." Taylor said, "Aw shucks, that's five days in a row now. I'm going to have to start all over again." Maryjane asked, "What are you two talking about?" Ralph answered, "As I was saying Buddy was not marking his territory, Buddy is Taylor's art critic." Iky said, "That sure is a smart dog." Maryjane asked, "Taylor what doe's it means when Buddy takes a crap on your work of art?" Taylor answered, "He has to go to the bathroom."

When Iky and Bigfoot were kids they were out in the barn-playing hide go seek. Bigfoot was doing the hiding and Iky was doing the seeking. Iky was looking all over for Bigfoot but he couldn't find him. While Iky was standing there looking around it started raining on him. Iky looked up and Bigfoot was standing on the edge of the loft taking a leak on him. Iky went and got Dad and told him what Bigfoot had just done to him. Dad beat the living piss out of Bigfoot. Bigfoot never done that to Iky again. Talk about a golden shower!

Whenever Jimbob Blowme goes to an Impact Team meeting, he always wears his special pants. The pants have a zipper in the rear end. Jerkbob East doesn't even wear any pants or underwear at the meetings and that is the bare facts.

The last major manic episode Iky had he had to spend three days in the local county jail. From there he was sent to the state mental hospital in Little Rock, Arkansas. The doctors got Iky back on track with new medications and group therapy as well. The counselors and hospital staff were wonderful. Iky made new friends with the other patients who were there. After spending five days at the mental hospital, Iky had his psychiatrist's permission to go home. Iky didn't have a way to get home, so the hospital provided him with transportation. The driver who drove Iky home was the Van Man, and he was a cool dude. While they were on the road, Van Man put on a CD. While they were listening to the music Iky asked, "Who's that group? They are awesome." Van Man answered, "That is my band."

When they drove up to Iky's mailbox, they took a right turn, as the Van Man started driving down the last three quarters of mile drive to Iky's house; the road was too rough for the van to make it. Iky said, "I can walk the rest of the home." Iky got out and thanked the Van Man. As he turned around and started walking the Van Man yelled, "Iky, come back here!" Iky turned around and walked back to him. Van Man asked, "Where are your shoes?" Iky was bare foot and he answered, "They are down at the police station, but hey don't worry about it. If Jesus could walk on water I can walk on land." Iky turned around and walked all the way home bare foot. There really is no place like home.

When Toots was growing up, she really had a bad temper and she still does. Like the time when Alex, Iky, and Bigfoot were playing king of the hill. There was a great big tree, which had fallen over on its side. Two people would get up on the tree at a time, trying to push the other one off. Whoever was standing after a battle would take on the other person who was watching. Toots walked up and saw what was going on, she wanted to try it. Bigfoot was the king of the hill at that moment. Toots got up on the tree and they started battling. Bigfoot pushed her off and Toots landed on the ground. Well, Alex and Iky were laughing there asses off, and that just fueled the fire because Toots was madder than a hornets nest.

Bigfoot jumped off the tree and standing there. When Toots picked herself up, she charged Bigfoot. She was swinging, kicking, and clawing at Bigfoot. He reached out and grabbed her ponytail with his left hand, than he pulled her head down and came up with about five or six stiff right hand upper cuts into her face. When Bigfoot let go of her hair Toots ran up to the house bawling. That reminds me of when restaurants used to have cubes of sugar they would ask you, while you were drinking a cup of coffee, "Do you want to have one lump or two?" Toots had about five lumps on her head. How sweet it is.

Carol Flatchest is so dumb she thinks that Wastewater Treatment is whenever you flush the toilet.

Many years have gone by since Iky and Death got their divorce. Death was laying on the couch all cuddled up with her new boyfriend, and as they were watching television a Coppertone commercial came on the screen. There was a beautiful looking babe lying on a beach, and this handsome looking young stud was rubbing Coppertone sunscreen lotion all over her body. Death asked her new boyfriend, "Wouldn't you like to be doing that to me?" The boyfriend answered, "Sure, do you have a paint roller."

Death jumped up off the couch and yelled, "I can't believe you said that to me!" Boyfriend said, "If you don't have a paint roller, a paint sprayer works just as well." Death yelled, "How dare you say that to me!" Boyfriend said, "It took nerve, because the blindfold fell off." Death yelled, "Get out of my house!" Boyfriend said, "You need to rephrase that sentence, because this is my house. Now put your cloths back on, lard butt and take your blindfold with you. Don't let the double doors hit you in the ass on the way out" Death stormed out of the house. The boyfriend got on the phone and said, "Hey Iky this is Psycho. I loved it. She also liked that tape of yours with that commercial on it."

Many years ago, Iky's Uncle Gus and Aunt Maryann were staying over at Mom and Dad's house. That night after everybody had supper, Toots showed up with her boyfriend Evan. This joker was so ugly he looked just like the joker in the Bat Man movie, but only Evan was not wearing any make up. I guess Toots figured that by going out with ugly looking men, it just made her look better. While the grownups were in the living room having drinks, Toots was in the kitchen getting Evan something to eat. Gus yelled, "Hey Toots, don't feed him too much because you might tame him!" After Evan ate, Toots and Evan were going to take off. Gus walked up to Evan, shook his hand, and said, "Well Evan, it was nice meeting you, but I don't think I'll be seeing you again." Gus was right!

Jimbob Blowme thinks that a Tampax is a cowboy from Texas who moved to Tampa Bay.

When Iky was a little boy, Uncle Ed walked up to Iky and held his finger out. Ed said, "Pull my finger." Iky grabbed his finger and jerked it extremely hard; it knocked Ed off balance. He had to take about four fast running steps to keep from falling on his face. Iky could smell something and he asked, "What's that smell? Did you step in cow shit?" Ed answered, "No Iky, that's not cow shit. You pulled my finger too hard." Iky asked, "Do you want me to try it again?" Ed answered, "No, wait until I go change my underwear first."

When Maryjane came home from work one evening she said to Iky, "Road Runner called me at work." Road Runner is her nephew and he said, "Aunt Maryjane, I am going on my first date this weekend, and I am very excited." Maryjane said, "Road Runner I'm very happy for you. Now if you are going to have sex make sure that you wear a rubber." Road Runner said, "That is the last thing that is on my mind. I am not even interested in sex at this time." Maryjane said to Iky, "Well I am really happy for him." Iky said, "Road Runner is a very smart young man, not wanting to have sex on his first date." Maryjane asked, "Why is that?" Iky answered, "Because he wants to see what it is like when you are married first."

Whenever Jerkbob East goes to a Down Time meeting, he wears kneepads. Jimbob Blowme has kneepads sewed into his pants.

While Cave Man was over at Bigfoot's house, they were drinking beer and playing games on the Xbox. Bigfoot asked, "Cave Man, is little Logan potty trained yet?" Cave Man answered, "No he is not, we have tried everything imaginable that you could think of, and nothing has worked so far. Logan at times gets up on our bed and he pees on it. If you put a diaper on him, he takes it off and smears it on the walls. Most of the time he just craps and pisses on the floor."

Bigfoot said laughing, "Well as long as Logan is crapping and pissing on the floor, just think about all the money that you are saving on diapers. I think I've got a solution to your problem." Bigfoot told Cave Man what he had in mind. One week went by and Cave Man called Bigfoot up, "Hey uncle Bigfoot I want to thank you for your idea on how to potty train Logan. Logan is so smart that when he gets done crapping and pissing. He scoops it out of the litter box and then throws it away." Bigfoot was surprised and he said, "No shit."

Years ago, there was a traveling salesman. He had just passed this small country town in rural Arkansas called Pigs Knuckle. As he was driving up to an old farmhouse, the salesman glanced out into the field. There was a man out in the field humping a goat; what he saw shocked him. The salesman drove up to the farmhouse, got out of his car and ran up the door. There was a little girl looking out the screen door at him. The salesman said, "Pardon me, it is probably none of my business, but there is a man out in that field humping a goat!" Little Death says, "That's my Mom and Dad." The salesman said, "Maybe I can sell that old goat a blindfold!"

When Iky was just a little kid, the whole family was sitting around the kitchen table eating supper. Toots wasn't feeling very well that day. As she walked into the kitchen suddenly she puked, "Blah!" She was standing in a big puddle of puke. Toots was bare foot and she was crying. Iky burst out laughing and Toots shouted, "You shut up!" She puked again, "Blah!" Iky said, "Hey Toots that reminds me of what your last boyfriend said to you. He said," "Kiss me honey. I want to puke." Toots puked again. "Blah!" Iky said, "It's true!"

When Iky was at work, he was he was talking to Dominico and Crack Shack. Iky said, "Two weeks ago, I was forced to go to one of Carol Flatchest's suck ass team meetings. The name of the team was Continuous Improvement Team. She can no longer extract any good knowledge from her Brownnosers or Suck Asses that always go to these meetings. I figured that I would just say some stupid shit and this is what happened." Flatchest said at the meeting, "We have a problem with our capper fillers. It seems like it runs in cycles." Iky said, "No, the capper fillers do not run in cycles. They spin round and round like a washing machine." Flatchest said, "That's not what I'm talking about. It seems like every month the fillers on the night shift go through a four night period where most of the jars are gross under filled."

Iky said, "It's just that time of the month, when the product is gross" Flatchest asked, "What time is that?" Jerkbob answered, "That is when you have to go buy a Kotex." Flatchest asked, "What is a Kotex? Is that like a text message?" Iky answered, "No that is more like a personal message. I know why they are having gross under fills on the capper fillers at night, because I used to run them." Flatchest was all excited and asked Iky, "Well, what is the problem?" Iky answered, "I don't have a problem." Flatchest said, "I'm talking about the capper filler problem." Blowme said, "I think that we need to buy those people some Kotex's." Flatchest shouted, "Shut up you moron!" Jerkbob asked, "Which one?" Flatchest asked Iky, "Why are we having gross under fills on our capper fillers once a month, on the night shift for a period of four days in a row?" Iky answered, "It is the gravitational pull of the moon gases caused by the full moon." Flatchest said, "Thank you very much Iky." Flatchest stopped running product at night during a full moon.

Crack Shack and Dominico were laughing there asses off, Iky asked, "Do you really want to know what is funny about this story?" Dominico answered, "Let me guess. Flatchest took your idea and fuckin submitted it to fuckin Corporate. She got a big fuckin bonus and Iky got a fuckin one way ticket to fuckin Pallukaville." Crack Shack asked, "Where the hell is Pallukaville?" Dominico answered, "It is on this side of fuckin Hoboken, New Jersey." Crack Shack asked, "What is at Pallukaville?" Dominico answered, "That's where all the fuckin bums go." Crack Shack said laughing, "Iky didn't get a bonus; he got a boner up his ass. Did you guys see that stupid team that they are putting together that is on the board?" Iky said, "That was my second idea. Team Pussy and the team are already filled up with the lazy worthless pussies."

Iky says, "If you think about it blow jobs really suck."

Iky was getting ready to go to town one day Maryjane was using the last of her lip balm. It was a lip plumper called Sexy Mother Pucker. Maryjane said, "Iky since you are going to town stop by Crazy Pearl's and pick me up some Sexy Mother Pucker." Iky said, "Okay." When Iky got back, he walked into the house with a good young looking young stud following him. Maryjane was watching television. Iky said, "Maryjane, I would like you to meet Jim. He works at Crazy Earl's." Maryjane said, "Hello Jim, how long have you known Iky?" Jim answered, "Oh, I just met him about forty minutes ago. I am here for you." Maryjane shouted, "Iky you idiot! I told you to go to Crazy Pearl's and get me a Sexy Mother Pucker, not a Sexy Mother Fucker!"

Many years ago, Alex and his parents spent a weekend at Iky's parents place. Later in the evening, the kids were told to go to bed. Therefore, Alex, Bigfoot, and Iky went upstairs and they closed the bedroom door. While the parents were downstairs having a few drinks, they could hear a loud commotion going on up stairs. Dad yelled, "You better get your asses to bed!" Well, the commotion stopped and it was quiet for a while, then the noisy racket started again. Dad got up out of his chair and walked up the stairs to the bedroom. When he opened the door, Dad walked in real fast. They had the lights turned off and, all of a sudden, a pillow hit Dad along side his head. Alex said later, "That was the worst beating that I have ever had." Iky said, "Those pillow fights can really hurt."

Pamerrhoid Nobrains thinks that a blowjob is when you are blowing cigarette smoke out of somebody's ass. Carol Flatchest thinks that it is a person that blows up tires in a tire shop.

The Lazy Boy Gary Man has the biggest set of lips in the world. In fact, Mick Jagger the lead singer of the Rolling Stones had a lawsuit against Lazy Boy. Jagger claimed there was no way humanly possible that anybody could have bigger lips then him. Jagger claimed that Lazy Boy must have had a lip implant. Forensic specialists had examined Lazy Boy's lips and decided they were real. Lazy Boy is extremely allergic to bee stings so he had to carry his anti bee sting venom with him at all times. It is Preparation H because it helps shrink swelling.

Lazy Boy had four pints of blood in his lips, which is why he is kind of a slow learner because he didn't have much blood going to his brain. One time Lazy Boy put too much Preparation H on his lips because they were chapped. He had such a head rush from his lips shrinking so fast. All the extra blood that squeezed out of his lips rushed into portions of his brain that had never been used before, which was basically all of it. All of a sudden, Lazy Boy yelled out, "Eureka, I've got it! Two plus two is three!"

One morning Jerkbob East was brushing his teeth with his new electric dildo called The Big Boy; he choked to death while it was in his mouth. Jerkbob was standing outside the gates of heaven. When they called his name, Jerkbob followed an angel into a room, Jerkbob took a seat and the angel walked out and closed the door. He was in the room for about thirty minutes. The door opened and Saint Peter walked in and closed the door. Saint Peter sat down in his chair. There was a big desk in front of him. Saint Peter glanced up at Jerkbob while he was looking over Jerkbob's file. Jerkbob had sweat pouring off him and he was shaking like a leaf. Saint Peter asked, "Do you have any idea where you are at?"

Jerkbob answered, "I must be in hell because it is so hot in here." Then, Jerkbob started whining and sniveling like a pussycat, "I am sorry for all of the mean things that I have ever said and done in my life. Especially that time when my girlfriend was over at my parent's house. I took a pickle out of the refrigerator, and I used it as a dildo on her. Then I put it back into the refrigerator and my Mom ate it that night." Saint Peter said, "This is not hell, but I am going to send you back to earth." Jerkbob said, "Please do not sent me to hell." Saint Peter said, "I told you that I was going to send you to back to earth, not hell." Jerkbob said, "Thank you for giving me a second chance. It is so hot in here I thought that this was hell."

Saint Peter said, "The reason it is so hot in here is because my heavy duty air conditioning unit is broke down right now." Jerkbob asked, "Well, can you fix it?" Saint Peter answered, "Yes we can, that's why I'm sending you back to Earth, because I have hooked up some special electrical hardware on your soul, and you will be running my air conditioning from now on." Saint Peter whispered into Jerkbob's ear what he was expected to do." Jerkbob said, "I will not let you down." Saint Peter said, "You know what will happen to you if you do." Jerkbob disappeared and he was back on earth.

At that, moment Saint Peter's air conditioner kicked on full blast. It got so cold in the room that Saint Peter was wearing a winter coat. He tried to turn the unit down but it just kept on blowing out cold air. Finally, Saint Peter built a pipeline straight to hell. Have you ever herd that expression, "When hell freezes over?" That is exactly what happened. Jerkbob single handily destroyed hell all by himself. I am sure you are wondering how he did it. Every time Jerkbob jerked off was the power source and he was working overtime. Jerkbob was even selling power back to the electric companies. He put the Energizer Bunny out of business. That is just like that old saying, "The Lord works in mysterious ways."

Iky was working in the dry ingredients room mixing up ingredients for the product they were running for that day. Iky's partner was Sal. Iky and Sal would mix up the flours, starches, sugar, and extra stuff in the big tank. When the people in the kitchen were ready for the dry ingredients, they would turn a light switch on that would light up on the control panel in the dry ingredients room. They turned the pump on and sent the batch to the kitchen, and then made up a new batch. Everyday the Q.C. woman named Connie would take a sample of the first batch, and take it back to the lab where it was tested and analyzed.

Sal said, "One day, Luke and I had our first batch made up, then we waited for Connie. Right then she walked into the room with her tray and sample cups. Luke had taken his hands and dipped them into the gooey product. When Connie walked up to him, Luke said, "Can you help me out here? My hands are all messed up and I have something in my pocket that I need to get out right now." She reached into his pocket and grabbed something and pulled on it, well it must have been stuck because it did not come out. After she pulled on it for about five or six more times, apparently it was making it get bigger.

She looked at Luke and he had a great big smile on his face. She let go of the thing that was in his pocket. Connie grabbed her tray and ran up front. Luke had pulled his right pants pocket out and he cut it out with his knife. Luke had a great big hard on and had it positioned inside his pants pocket." Iky said, "I know why Connie ran up front." Sal asked, "Why?" Iky answered, "Because she went to go get a longer pool stick and a pool rack to rack his balls." Sal said, "Maybe Connie was getting some quarters so that she could play pocket pool." Iky said, "Well Connie would have to put the quarters in Luke's other pocket." Sal asked. "Why?" Iky answered, "Because that way the change wouldn't fall through the hole that was in his pocket."

When Iky was a kid, growing up at home one day the cow got out into the neighbors field. Iky and Dad had to cross the fence to get to the cow. They walked up to the cow and Dad put a rope round its neck. While they were walking the cow back home, the big dog named

Oris ran up to the cow and went, "Ruff!" It scared the cow and it took off running. The rope pulled out of Dad's hand, and than it wrapped around his leg. The cow pulled Dad off his feet, and the running cow was dragging Dad; he was bouncing up and down on his butt. When the cow got to the fence, it started smashing its way through. Dad finally got the rope off his leg. Dad jumped up he pulled his pistol out of the holster, pointed the gun at Oris, and fired a shot. Dad missed and Oris ran all the way home. Iky didn't dare to laugh.

When Carol Flatchest got her Manager's job at the factory, Flatchest and her husband bought a very nice house in a quiet residential neighborhood. The first morning the milkman delivered milk to them; he walked up to the house and knocked on the door. Flatchest opened up the door and she was only wearing her panties and a new support bra. The support bra consisted of two half-inch squares of duck tape. When the milkman looked at her he asked, "Is your wife home? I would like to welcome her to the neighborhood." Flatchest answered, "I do not have a wife but I have a husband." The milkman asked, "Can you go get him for me?" Flatchest answered, "Okay." She went back into the house and her husband went to the door. He said, "My wife said that you wanted to talk to me." The milkman slapped him and then handed him a Philippine mail order bride catalog. The milkman said, "You have my sympathy." He closed the door and never went back.

Psycho's Nephew Jimmy was spending the weekend with him. Jimmy said, "I have a very important question that I would like to ask you." Psycho said, "Well, go ahead and ask me." Jimmy said, "I feel kind of embarrassed to even ask it." Psycho said, "There is no need to be embarrassed of anything, so go ahead and ask me your question." Jimmy asked, "How old were you when you quit jacking off?" Psycho answered, "Why would you want to quit a good thing?"

When Maryjane worked for the city, she was in her office one day working on the computer. Well, the Assistant Director of her department named Mack Pillion walked into her office. For all of you older people like myself in our generations there was no such thing as an assistant. The only true purpose of having an assistant now days in management is to use them as the fall guy to protect the director above them. Their main purpose is to bring the director coffee and doughnuts. Mack was in Maryjane's office griping at her. Mack was just like a hole in one; in other words, he was an asshole. When Mack was finally finished with his gripe session, Maryjane said, "Mack, I really appreciate your important input since we get so very little of it around here." Those were words very well spoken. Mack walked out and never came back.

Jerkbob East thinks that a Kotex is two cowboys from Texas.

Iky has a unique way of turning things around on people who like to laugh and use him up. Like the time when Toots was married to her second husband Ricky Dickey. Bigfoot and Iky stopped over at their place, and while they were all sitting around the kitchen table, they were telling stories about the childhood days growing up. Toots said, "Hey Bigfoot, do you remember that time when Iky ate a worm?" I am going to get the record straight on this issue. Toots and Bigfoot found an earthworm. Toots dared Iky to eat it. Well Iky took it and bit it in half, and than he threw the two halves down on the ground. A dare is a dare but he did not eat it. Now back to the story.

Toot's stepdaughter Trixy asked, "Iky did you eat a worm?" Iky answered. "No I did not eat a worm." Toots said very loudly, "Yes you did!" Then Toots and Trixy started singing and laughing at Iky, "Iky ate a worm, Iky ate a worm!" Iky said, "Yeah Toots, you have eaten countless worms all your life, and you are still eating them to this day." Toots said, "You tell me when I have ever eaten a worm!" Iky answered very loudly, "Every time that you have given a guy a blow job!" Trixy asked, "What's a blow job?" Bigfoot answered, "That's when you blow on a night crawler." Trixy asked, "What is a night crawler?" Iky answered, "That is a great big long one eyed wonder worm that comes out at night." Now Trixy and Iky are singing and laughing at Toots, "Toots is eating worms, Toots is eating worms!" While Toots was sitting there, her face was beet red, and she was biting her worm I mean her lip.

Iky asked, "Toots, do you have any extra night crawlers that I can use for fishing today?" Trixy answered, "No, because she ate them last night.

By the way, how long do you have to blow on the night crawlers?" Iky answered, "I really don't know. I have never had anybody blow on my night crawler. You are going to have to ask Toot's that question." Right then Toots stood up, walked into her bedroom and closed the door. Trixy said, "She must be looking for the night crawlers." Iky said, "No, she must be looking for her worm medicine." Trixy said, "The worm medicine is down in the dog kennel." Iky said, "No, she is looking for that other worm medicine that is in the bedroom." Trixy asked, "What is that worm medicine called?" Bigfoot answered, "Viagra."

Trixy asked, "What does Viagra do?" Iky answered, "It makes your night crawler get big so that you can blow on it." Toots walked out of the bedroom, went outside, got into her truck, and drove to the casino. While we thought Toots was in the bedroom, she was actually in the bathroom washing her mouth out with Listerine. Trixy said, "I'll bet you she went to the bait shop to get some Viagra." Iky asked, "Why would she go the bait shop to get some Viagra?" Trixy answered, "Because that is where the night crawlers are at. Oh, by the way how big do those one eyed wonder worms get when you blow on them?" Iky answered, "I don't know. It probably depends on how long you blow on them. You will have to ask Toots that question when she gets back, because Toots likes to eat worms."

I kind of feel that this joke is appropriate at this time. When Iky was a kid the whole family was sitting at the kitchen table eating supper. People from the North eat supper at six o'clock at night. Every year Iky's family would plant a great big garden. That night Mom had cooked a big head of cauliflower. Iky took a piece of cauliflower and put it on his plate. While he was eating, Iky took his fork and cut into the cauliflower. All of a sudden, Iky yelled, "There's a worm looking at me!" There was a great big cooked green worm looking at Iky. Well nobody ate any of that cauliflower. I guess Iky should have gave Toots that worm, since she liked to eat worms.

One day at work while Five Beers and Iky were out in the plant working, this very attractive looking woman was walking through the plant. Five Beers said to Iky, "Man I would sure like to screw that." Iky turned to see whom Five Beers was talking about; the attractive looking babe had just walked behind a big dumpster. Now walking out from the other end of the dumpster was Gah Gah. He was not a person, but more of a what. Iky asked, "Who, Gah Gah?" Five Beers punched Iky in his arm and said, "Iky, you are sick." Iky said, "How could you possibly call me sick? I'm not the one who wants to screw Gah Gah!"

When Iky and Psycho were at the Springdale Gun Show, they were talking to a man named Norse whom had a table set up. Iky asked Norse, "Have you been in the service?" Norse answered, "Yes, I was in the Army from 1961 to 1969. I remember when I was in Vietnam. My buddy Mark and I were sitting in our foxholes. We were watching a B-52 raid from a distance, and as they were carpet-bombing a large area and blowing it to hell, Mark said, "You know, if I would have just learned something in school, I could be dropping those bombs right now." I told him, "If I would have just learned something in school, I would be making those B-52's." Psycho said, "I did not learn anything in school because I already knew it." After thinking for a while Iky said, "Well at least I learned how to wipe my ass in school."

Norse said, "Most College grads can't even do that today." Iky said, "I think that I am going to go to College and get me a diploma so that I can get a better job." Psycho said, "Iky, they have a saying in college while you are sitting on a toilet that goes, "The job is not finished until the paper work is done." Iky said, "No shit." Norse said, "In college they have the constipation poem too." Iky asked, "Don't you mean constitution poem?" Norse answered, "Well it's kind of like that and it goes, "Here I sit broken hearted came to shit but only farted." Psycho said, "That reminds me of what Benjamin Franklin's last words were while he was on his death bed."

Iky interrupted Psycho and said, "He said get me the hell out of here!" Norse said, "That was Saddam Insane's last words." Iky said, "No Saddam's last words were while they were putting the rope around his neck." He said, "Tell the world that I am well hung." He actually had twelve inches." Psycho said, "Anyway, back to Benjamin Franklin." Iky interrupted Psycho again and asked, "Didn't he invent maple syrup?"

Norse answered, "No that was Aunt Jamima." Iky said, "Yeah that's right they had slaves back then." Psycho yelled, "Shut the hell up and let me finish my story!" Norse asked Iky, "What's his problem?" Iky answered, "Aw nothing out of the ordinary, he's just Psycho." Psycho finally said, "Benjamin Franklin's last words were "Fart proudly." Iky said, "I like that. Oh, by the way who was Benjamin Franklin?" Norse answered, "He was Aunt Jamima's nephew."

Jerkbob East said to Jimbob Blowme, "Sex just doesn't seem to interest me lately," Jimbob said, "Sometimes it helps if you switch hands." Jerkbob said, "I don't know if that would really work. Because the last time that I was playing cards I had a royal flush." Jerkoff is the jack-off-of-all-trades.

Iky's Dad grew up on a farm, but when he was eighteen Dad moved to Los Angeles and stayed with his uncle. That summer Dad got a job working for Hormel. There were many women working at the plant, and they would pester Dad and try to embarrass him. Sometimes they would pinch him on his butt and other places too. They would say dirty things to him, like what they wanted to do to him, and make him blush. One day Dad was talking to someone, and a very attractive looking woman walked by. She reached out and grabbed Dad's butt. Then she smiled at him and kept on walking. Dad said, "I sure would like to screw that." The person he was talking to laughed and said, "Yeah, she is outstanding in bed." Dad asked, "So you have tried her out?" Guy answered, "Hell yeah I have! She's my wife!" Dad said that he had never been so embarrassed in his life.

The first and last time that Death ever cooked for Iky, she cooked him a TV dinner. Iky ate everything on the plate including the plate itself. She was proud that she cooked it all by herself without having any help from her boyfriends. When Death gave Iky the dinner Iky said, "Thank you, but you are supposed to cook the dinner in the microwave oven first. Iky gave her back the frozen dinner and she finally cooked it.

After Iky finished eating the dinner, Death asked, "Well, how was it?" Iky answered, "Do you want to know the truth?" Death said, "Well yeah." Iky said, "It wasn't worth a shit." Death asked, "Then why did you eat it?" Iky answered, "Because I was hungry." Iky was happy that she finally quit cooking. Iky was getting extremely too much fiber in his diet from eating the boxes the TV dinners came in. Whenever Death's mother Dumbass cooked TV dinners, she threw the whole box and all into the oven. Then Dumbass usually forgot to turn the oven on. She was such a dingbat that she would go to the golf course and bring home golf balls thinking they were giant white pearls. Shame thought they were chicken eggs and ate them for breakfast.

Many years ago, Iky went to Bismarck, North Dakota and he spent a few days at Uncle Gus and Aunt Maryann's farm. Back then, Gus was a fulltime farmer. Gus was worried that it was going to rain the next day, because he was going to spray his neighbor's field. If it rained, he would not be able to spray and this would set him back. That evening Gus went to bed worried. While Maryann and Iky were in the kitchen talking Gus walked into the kitchen. He was only wearing a pair of boxer shorts. He had a blank looking stare on his face, and then he started scratching his balls. Gus said, "Where's the weeds and the trees?"

Iky said, "Hey, Gus what are you doing?" Maryann said, "Be quiet, he's sleepwalking." Gus said again, "Where's the weeds and the trees?" Gus scratched his balls some more then he walked into the living room and he stood there taking a leak on a fake tree in a planter. When Gus finished he went back to bed. Maryann said, "That means that it is going to rain tomorrow. Gus can predict the weather by doing that and the funny thing about it is, he doesn't even remember doing it."

Iky said, "Meteorologists use a term for what Gus was doing." Maryann asked, "What's that?" Iky answered, "That is called relative humidity." Iky sat there thinking for a while and asked, "Maryann, what does it mean if Gus takes a crap on the living room floor?" Maryann answered, "It means three things. First, it is time to fertilize the fields.

Second, he has to clean it up, and the third thing is that he doesn't get any supper."

Then, Gus sleepwalked back into the kitchen. He was standing there scratching his balls and his ass, not saying anything. He turned around and walked back into the bedroom. Iky said, "I guess Gus was just telling us what time it is." Maryann asked, "What time is that?" Iky answered, "It's half past the monkey's ass according to his balls."

One year when Iky was in North Dakota, he bought a car and brought it back to Arkansas. The first day he drove the car to work, Jerkbob and Blowme were out in the parking lot. They saw Iky drive up and park the car. The two morons noticed there was an electric cord dangling in front the radiator. Most northern vehicles have what they call a tank heater. You plug it in during the cold winter months to warm up your engine block so your car will start. Jerkbob said, "Hey Iky's got one of them new electric cars." Blowme asked, "Iky, where did you get that electric car?" Iky answered, "I bought it while I was in North Dakota." Jerkbob asked, "Do you get good mileage out of that car?" Iky answered, "That depends." Blowme asked, "Depends on what?" Iky answered, "It depends on how much electric cord you are willing to buy." Iky walked into the plant. Jerkbob said to Blowme, "Those electric cars cost too much to run." Blowme asked, "How do you figure that?" Jerkbob answered, "Because Iky's car is not plugged in, and he must have left all of his electric cord on the road from here to North Dakota."

Iky thinks that Go-Jo is that ruthless rabble rousing Japanese War Minister from World War II.

Many years ago, Iky's Uncle Clarence and Oreo Coleman were sitting in a bar in Valley City, North Dakota getting gooned up. Clarence asked Oreo, "Would you screw my wife?" Oreo answered, "Only if she needed it." Clarence hauled off and knocked Oreo off his bar stool. Many years later when Oreo told Iky that story, Iky asked Oreo, "Why didn't you just tell Clarence that you wouldn't screw her?" Oreo answered, "Because I told Clarence that the first time when he asked me that question. Then he knocked me out the front door of the bar." Iky said, "Sometimes silence is golden."

Iky was over at Meano's house one day. While they were drinking beer and getting drunk, it started piss-pouring rain outside. Meano looked out the window and said, "Look at this, Iky." There was a guy carrying a table over his head. Iky said, "I know what that guy is doing." Meano asked, "What are you taking about Iky?" Iky answered, "That guy is using an Arkie umbrella."

Iky thinks in order to straighten this country up and to keep people from going further in debt, there should be no more credit and everything should be based on a cash and carry system. This is a very simple system. If you do not have the cash then you do not carry.

The Lazy Boy Gary Man is the only person in the plant who has another person assigned to help him. If you pull out his bid slip, it is in writing that John Lawton is required to do all of Lazy Boy's work. John's requirements are:

1. Help Lazy Boy change into his work clothes.

2. Drive Lazy Boy to the time clock, so that John can clock him in.

3. Drive Lazy Boy to the break room, so he can have his four-hour break before he starts work.

4. Drive back to break room, pick Lazy Boy up, and set him into the buggy. Then drive Lazy Boy back to the time clock where John clocks him out for lunch.

5. Drive to cafeteria so Lazy Boy can have his four-hour lunch break.

6. Drive back to cafeteria pick Lazy Boy up and set him into the buggy. Then drive Lazy Boy back to the time clock where John clocks him out. Drive Lazy Boy to the locker room.

7. Carry Lazy Boy into locker room.

8. Help Lazy Boy, change back into his street clothes.

9. John is required to go back to work for eight more hours so that he can do his own job.

10. Sign Lazy Boy's pay checks once a week.

Just like the old saying that is not used anymore, "John has a Porch Monkey on his back.

Carol Flatchest is so dumb that she thinks Obama's stimulus package plan is free samples of Viagra and Niagara, for every red blooded American who needs them.

When Iky had his first major manic episode in 2001, he was sent to the Fort Smith hospital. There he was diagnosed with Bipolar Disorder. Iky spent several days at the hospital. At that time, there were many other patients. Some were suffering from Schizophrenia, Bipolar, Severe Depression, and other many other mental illnesses. If you think that you have a rough life, you should go to one of these hospitals and see what these people experience on a daily basis. At least they were able to get help.

Those who do not get help can suffer tragic consequences, like what happened to a patient named Jimmy. The story Jimmy told Iky while he was at the hospital was so heart breaking it will probably make you cry because Iky did. You might want to have a box of Kleenex Tissue handy when you read this story because you will need it. Jimmy said, "I was at my home all alone when the manic episode came over me. I was sitting in my recliner and the television was turned off. I was beginning to panic; I had nobody to talk to or help me through the horrible episode that I was having. I asked God, "Please help me. God, I need you more than ever."

Jimmy continued, "Right then the television turned on as if by magic. George Bush was on the television screen, and I had a very long intelligent conversation with him. George Bush saved my life." Iky said, "Jimmy I hate to tell you this but that did not happen." Jimmy asked, "Why not?" Iky answered, "Because nobody has ever had an intelligent conversation with George Bush." Jimmy said, "Maybe it was Dick Cheney."

When Death was married to her first husband, she walked into the bathroom and caught Rick the Dick masturbating. Death yelled, "That is disgusting! I'm going to call my Momma and Daddy and tell them what you are doing!" While he was taking the blind fold off, Rick said, "Tell Shame I'm through with his blindfold and he can have it back. Oh one more thing, I wasn't fantasizing about you! By the way, Death, I feel like Sam Pecking paw dunkin doughnuts! Would you like to have this last box of homemade glazed doughnuts that have nuts on them? You have been eating them ever since we got married and your parents like them too! Oh and by the way, the secret hidden ingredient in your hidden valley ranch is that doughnut glaze also! Now I want a divorce!" Death said, "But I like those glazed doughnuts with nuts on them."

When Iky's family moved to Minnesota, Iky's parents went to the neighbors' house to introduce themselves. Dad knocked on the door and out came Ole and Lena. Dad looked at Lena and said, "My God, you are a big woman." Lena said, "I am six veet vour and weigh two hundred and vifty pounds." Dad said, "You ought to be playing with the Green Bay Packers." Lena put her arm around Ole and said, "No thank you, I only play with Ole's packer."

One day Jimbob Blowme was at a Continuous Improvements Team meeting. At the meeting, the discussion was about how they could eliminate all unnecessary overtime, wasteful spending, and misuse of company funds. While all of the team members were sitting in their brand new recliners, some were watching a football game on the companies brand new big screen television. Others were checking porn websites on the brand new computers, eating freshly delivered pizza and drinking beer. Jerkbob said, "It doesn't get any better than this." Blowme said, "What I really like about these team meetings is that we get paid time and a half." Jerkbob said, "I think that we should take away the employee's retirement, medical, dental, and vacation benefits. That will save the company lots of money." Blowme said, "We have already done that. That is why we can have these team meetings."

Jerkbob said, "I really like that new gay channel." Blowme asked, "Which one?" Jerkbob answered, "That Playboy channel."

One day Pamerrhoid Nobrains walked out to the mailbox, and there was a stray dog in her yard. She talked it over with her husband and they decided to take it to the humane society. As Nobrains and her husband walked into the building with the dog, a worker named Thomas walked up to them. He petted Nobrains on the head and said, "We might be able to find a home for you old boy." Nobrains said, "But I already have a home." Nobrains husband Hemorrhage said, "That is my wife!" Thomas said, "You have my sympathy, and does she have her rabies shots? Would you take a walk with me?"

Thomas and Hemorrhage left for about twenty minutes. When they got back, Hemorrhage took the dog home and left Nobrains there. Thomas said, "Follow me Nobrains." As they were heading further back into the building Nobrains asked, "How long have you worked here Thomas?" Thomas answered, "I've been here for two and a half years." Nobrains said, "You look familiar." Thomas said, "Go into this room." Nobrains walked in and as Thomas was closing the door he said, "By the way, my nickname is Psycho and you framed me and fired me. Go ahead and turn on the gas, Iky!"

Psycho closed the door. After two hours of gassing, Nobrains lived. Psycho drove over to Hemorrhage's house and gave him his money back and a box of Milk Bone dog biscuits. Psycho took his dog back and said, "Go get Nobrains. She is at the city dog pound. She likes those biscuits and the gassing didn't work either." Actually, the gas made Nobrains get smart because she yelled out, "I figured out how the maintenance men get down from the roof of the plant after they have used the staircase to get up there. They use a parachute to get back down!" She must be related to Rasputin!"

Did you notice that Dick Cheney was in a wheel chair at Obama's inauguration? They claim that he hurt himself by lifting some boxes while he was moving out of the White House. What really happened was that when the Clintons stole everything out of the White House, when Hillary, I mean Bill left office, the secret service bolted everything down in the White House. When Dick Cheney told George Bush to load the big table in the oval office into his U hall, George said, "Do it yourself, you're not my commandeering chief anymore." Dick hurt himself trying to get that table that would not budge. In fact when the Clintons left the White House they put a for sale sign out in front of it. That was because they could not take it with them.

When Iky's dad Raymond was a little kid, Oreo Coleman gave him a nickel so that he would push his best friend Denny Denison down a coal shoot. When Raymond's parents found out what he had done, his Mom asked him, "Why did you do that? That was a mean thing that you did to Denny." Raymond answered, "Oreo gave me a nickel to do it." Raymond's Dad said, "I guess the price has gone up over the years." Mom asked, "What are you talking about?" Dad answered. "When I was a kid I got paid a penny to push Oreo down the same coal shoot."

Jerkbob East, the workplace bully is so dumb he said to Iky, "The Stone Age was during the 1960's, when the hippies, peace protesters, flower children, and pussy pacifists who would not fight back. We're all getting stoned on pot at that time and they sat around singing, cum by yaw my lord cum by yaw." Jerkbob also said, "That is you Iky." He stood there laughing at Iky with a stupid look on his face. Maybe some day Jerkbob can sing along with that song when someone sings it to him. Just like the way he sung it to Iky and the countless other people at work who he relentlessly harassed. Jerkbob thinks that he is a real bad ass, but in reality, he is nothing but a dumb ass. Jerkbob always said his motto is, "No Mercy."

The only thing that is bad about Jerkbob is his breath, especially when he is drinking. If he breathes on you, you may be pulled over for second hand booze breath. That is, if you do not pass out first. Jerkbob, Iky would like to thank you for everything that you have done for him, especially when you accidentally knocked him into the lockers in the locker room. When Iky spun around and looked you right in your eyes, you said, "Oh, I did not see you." Iky replied, "You better open your eyes so you can see where you are going."

Iky would also like to thank the Assistant Human Resources Director Jimbob Blowme, the Human Resources Director Pamerrhoid Nobrains, the Cereal Production Manager Asshwipe Schmidt, and last but not least, the Plant Manager Carol Flatchest. All of you people were protecting Jerkoff and making everybody's jobs and home life miserable by creating your hostile work environment in the plant. If it had not been for you Management Knuckle Heads, Iky would still be at work and not disabled. Asshwipe Schmidt, it is funny you told Iky that he could lose his job after he reported Jerkbob had assaulted him. Then later on Jerkoff slandered Iky. Take Iky's job and shove it. Iky aint working there no more. Jerkoff was bragging that he was going to make Iky snap.

Iky can take it because now Iky sits at home, writing short stories and jokes. Iky gets his Government check once a month. Now Iky has the most important thing in life, and that is time. It is just like that Rolling Stones song, "I got time on my side." Oh by the way, how much time did it take the Management Knuckle Heads, to find new jobs after the company finally fired them all? I have also heard that Jerkbob East had a sex change operation and it was a success. Now Jerkbob is finally a man for a change. That is why the company has made him a lead man, which was why he had his sex change. They tried to break Iky's spirit, but they could never touch his soul.

Psycho asked Iky, "What ever happened to that ex wife of yours named Death?" Iky answered, "Well, as the years have gone by, I have heard that her boob job is sagging. The tummy roll and tuck has broken loose, the facelift has turned into a mudslide. Her butt looks like the Himalayans; him no longer laying no more. She smells like a bankrupt rotten sperm bank that has gone out of business. The blindfold does not work anymore, because whenever she suggests someone use it they all say, "Where's my gas mask, cigarette and firing squad?"

"The fancy jewelry and clothes have no appeal anymore. She used to put her feet behind her ears to try to attract men. Now the only thing it attracts is flies. Whenever she accuses anybody of looking at other women, after looking at her they all say, "You bet I am." She doesn't even have her own pot to piss in; Death is living in her own living hell. She always thought that she was a beauty queen, but now she is nothing more than a scum queen."

"Men used to take her out and wine and dine her. Now the only place they take her to is the dog kennel. Just like that ACDC song, "Giving the dog a bone." Her lying, cheating, and stealing have finally caught up to her." While he was laughing his ass off, Psycho said, "That is the true agony of defeat." Iky said, "There is a moral to all of her stories." Psycho asked, "What is the moral?" Iky answered, "Love is truly blind when you are wearing a blindfold." Psycho said, "I think I'm going to laugh myself to death."

Iky says, "If you finally reach the point in your life where you can no longer laugh, than it is time to go to the Funny Farm."

When it comes to joke telling, the best jokes are the ones where you
laugh with somebody, not at them. Just like the old sayings:
No mercy.
Paybacks are a mother.
What goes around comes around.
Revenge is a dish best served cold.
An eye for an eye, and a tooth for a tooth.
Give a man enough rope and he will hang himself.
What does not kill you in life will make you stronger.
Good thing's always happens to those who choose to wait.
Sticks and stones may break my bones but words can never hurt me.
Do unto others, as you would like them to do unto you.
There is a difference between revenge and justice.
"Vengeance is mine, I shall repay." Romans 12:19.

Iky the Jew.

About the author, Randy Cassatt was born in Valley City, North Dakota on March 28, 1961. His family moved to a farm north of Detroit Lakes, Minnesota in 1966. While Randy was in high school, he took up amateur boxing. After graduating high school in 1980, Randy moved to Fort Smith, Arkansas. In 1985, he won the Western Arkansas and Eastern Oklahoma Tough Man Contest. He now resides in Rudy, Arkansas.